Seal of the State of Idaho

CHRONOLOGY AND DOCUMENTARY HANDBOOK OF THE STATE OF IDAHO

ROBERT I. VEXLER

State Editor

WILLIAM F. SWINDLER

Series Editor

1978 OCEANA PUBLICATIONS, INC./Dobbs Ferry, New York

Library of Congress Cataloging in Publication Data

Main entry under title:

Chronology and documentary handbook of the State of Idaho.

  (Chronologies and documentary handbooks of the States;
v. 12)
    Bibliography: p.
    Includes index.
    SUMMARY: Contains a chronology of historical events
from 1805 to 1977, a biographical directory of prominent citizens,
and copies of pertinent documents.
    1. Idaho — History — Chronology. 2. Idaho —
Biography. 3. Idaho — History — Sources. [1. Idaho —
History] I. Vexler, Robert I. II. Series.
F746.C47   979.6   78-6092
ISBN 0-379-16137-0

Manufactured in the United State of America

TABLE OF CONTENTS

ACKNOWLEDGMENT

Special recognition should be accorded Melvin Hecker, whose research has made a valuable contribution to this volume.

Thanks to my wife, Francine, in appreciation of her help in the preparation of this work.

Thanks also to my children, David and Melissa, without whose patience and understanding I would have been unable to devote the considerable time necessary for completing the state chronology series.

Robert I. Vexler

INTRODUCTION

This projected series of <u>Chronologies and Documentary Handbooks of the States</u> will ultimately comprise fifty separate volumes - one for each of the states of the Union. Each volume is intended to provide a concise ready reference of basic data on the state, and to serve as a starting point for more extended study as the individual user may require. Hopefully, it will be a guidebook for a better informed citizenry - students, civic and service organizations, professional and business personnel, and others.

The editorial plan for the <u>Handbook</u> series falls into six divisions: (1) a chronology of selected events in the history of the state; (2) a short biographical directory of the principal public officials, e.g., governors, Senators and Representatives; (3) a short biographical directory of prominent personalities of the state (for most states); (4) the first state constitution; (5) the text of some representative documents illustrating main currents in the political, economic, social or cultural history of the state; and (6) a selected bibliography for those seeking further or more detailed information. Most of the data found in the present volume, in fact, have been taken from one or another of these references.

The current constitutions of all fifty states, as well as the federal Constitution, are regularly kept up to date in the definitive collection maintained by the Legislative Drafting Research Fund of Columbia University and published by the publisher of the present series of <u>Handbooks</u>. These texts are available in most major libraries under the title, <u>Constitutions of the United States: National and State</u>, in two volumes, with a companion volume, the <u>Index Digest of State Constitutions</u>.

Finally, the complete collection of documents illustrative of the constitutional development of each state, from colonial or territorial status up to the current constitution as found in the Columbia University collection, is being prepared for publication in a multi-volume series by the present series editor. Whereas the present series of <u>Handbooks</u> is intended for a wide range of interested citizens, the series of annotated constitutional materials in the volumes of <u>Sources and Documents of U. S. Constitutions</u> is primarily for the specialist in government, history or law. This is not to suggest that the general citizenry may not profit equally from referring to these materials; rather, it points up the separate purpose of the <u>Handbooks</u>, which is to guide the user to these and other sources of authoritative information with which he may systematically enrich his knowledge of this state and its place in the American Union.

William F. Swindler
Series Editor

Robert I. Vexler
Series Associate Editor

Mayest Thou Endure Forever

State Motto

CHRONOLOGY

1805 Meriwether Lewis and William Clark explored Idaho. The site of Fort Lemhi in what is now Lemhi County was the rendezvous for two divisions of the expedition after which they united and later reached the south fork of the Clearwater River.

1810 The Missouri Fur Company established Fort Henry on the Snake River.

1811 The Pacific Fur Company sponsored an expedition which descended the Snake River to the Columbia.

1819 February 8. Jerome County was created and named for Jerome Hill. Jerome is the county seat.

1834 Fort Hall in what is now Bingham County was founded. It became the meeting point of several trails which led to the western parts of North America.

1836 Henry Spalding founded a mission at Lapwai.

1846 August 5. Idaho was acquired by the United States as part of the American territory agreed to in the Webster-Ashburton Treaty between the United States and Great Britain.

1848 Idaho was made a part of the Territory of Oregon and continued as such until 1853.

1853 The southern part of the state remained in Oregon Territory. The northern part was made a portion of Washington Territory. This territorial division continued until 1859.

1855 The town of Mullan was founded where the wagon road crossed the Coeur d'Alene Mountains. It was named for Joseph Mullan.

1856 The Coeur d'Alenes, Palouses and Spokanes went on the war path.

1857 April. The Coeur d'Alenes, Palouses and Spokanes fought with troops commanded by Colonel Edward Jenner Steptoe, causing the latter to take flight. Colonel George Wright led a punitive expedition against the Indian tribes and successfully defeated them.

1859   Idaho became part of Washington Territory
            and remained in this territorial division
            until 1863.

1860   April 14. Mormons founded the first perma-
            nent settlement in Idaho at Franklin.

            September 30. Gold was discovered on Oro-
            fino Creek.

1862   August. The Golden Age was the first news-
            paper to be published in Idaho at Lewiston.
            It continued publication until January,
            1865.

            Late summer or autumn. The first effort was
            made to gain a territorial organization for
            Idaho at Oro Fino, the mining town located
            east of Lewiston.

            December 23. Dispensation was granted to
            William Kaufman, Frederick G. Schwatka,
            Frederick H. Simmons and others to found a
            masonic lodge at Lewiston. The lodge was
            chartered on November 26, 1863 after which
            it developed dissensions which led to a
            surrender of the charter on December 1, 1865.

1863   March 3. Congress passed the Organic Act
            creating the Territory of Idaho.

            March 4. The Territory of Idaho was estab-
            lished including Montana until 1864 and part
            of Wyoming until 1868.

            July 10. President Abraham Lincoln appointed
            William H. Wallace first governor of the
            Territory of Idaho.

            December 7. The first Territorial legisla-
            tive assembly met at Lewiston. The session
            lasted until February 4, 1864.

            December 31. Owyhee County was created.
            It was a corruption of Hawaii. Murphy is
            the county seat.

            Latter Day Saints, followers of Joseph Morris
            who broke off from the main group of Mormons,
            and were called "Morrisites," settled at
            Soda Springs.

1864   January 22. Oneida County was created. It

was named for Oneida, New York, which in
turn had been named for the Oneida Indians.
Malad City is the county seat.

February 4. The following counties were
established: Boise with its county seat at
Idaho City, Idaho with its county seat at
Grangeville, Nez Perce with its county seat
at Lewiston, and Shoshone with its county
seat at Wallace. Nez Perce and Shoshone
Counties arenamed for the Nez Perce and
Shoshonean Indian tribes.

June 22. The second Masonic lodge was
chartered. Dispensation had been granted on
July 7, 1863 by the Oregon Grand Lodge for
this lodge to be established at Bannock.

July 26. The _Statesman_ was first issued as
a tri-weekly paper at Boise.

October 12. Governor Caleb Lyon, who served
as territorial governor until 1865, arrived
in Boise.

December 22. Ada, Kootenai and Latah Counties were created. Ada was named for Ada
Riggs, daughter of H. C. Riggs, one of the
founders of Boise, and Kootenai for the Kate-
nai Indian tribe. Boise is the county seat
of Ada County; Coeur d'Alene of Kootenai
County, and Moscow of Latah County.

December 24. Boise became the capital of
the Territory.

1865   August. J. L. Hardin and Joseph Wasson
            established the _Owybee Avalanche_ at Silver
            City.

            C. de Witt Smith was Secretary and Acting
            Governor of the Territory. He was succeeded
            in that position by Horace C. Gilson who
            served until 1866.

1866   S. R. Howlett was Secretary and Acting Gover-
            nor of the Territory. David W. Ballard was
            appointed governor and served until 1870.

1868   March 3. A Catholic Vicarate was established
            in Idaho. The Rt. Rev. Louis Lootens was
            assigned vicar apostolic.

August 9. Rt. Rev. Louis Looters was con-
secrated Bishop of Castabala. He served
until his resignation on July 16, 1876.

1869   January 9. Lemhi County with its county
            seat at Salmon was established. It was named
            for Limhi, a character in the Book of Mormon.

            A penitentiary was constructed at Boise under
            the supervision of Thomas Donaldson.

1870   E. J. Curtis was Acting Governor of the
            Territory of Idaho.

1871   Thomas W. Bennett became Governor of Idaho
            and served until 1875.

            Under an act of Congress Idaho was granted
            a law library of 500 volumes at a cost of
            approximately $2,500.

1872   Yellowstone National Park (consisting of
            parts of Idaho, Montana and Wyoming) was
            created. It contained 2,219,823 acres.

1873   The Interior Department established the
            Wallowa country as a reservation for the Lower
            Nez Perces.

1875   January 5. Bear Lake County was established
            with its county seat at Paris.

            D. P. Thompson became Governor of the terri-
            tory. He served until 1876.

1876   Mason Brayman became governor of Idaho Terri-
            tory and served until 1880.

1877   March 12. George W. McCrary became Secretary
            of War in the Cabinet of President Rutherford
            B. Hayes

            June 14. Chief Joseph led his Nez Perce
            tribes on the warpath. The Indians refused
            to settle on the reservation established for
            them. The Nez Perces along with the Bannock
            Indians continued to fight with United States
            troops until 1879.

1879   February 20. Cassia County with its county
            seat at Burley and Washington County with
            its seat at Weiser were established. Washing-
            ton was named for George Washington, first

President of the United States.

1880   Population: 32,610.

The railroad was completed to southeastern
Idaho.

John B. Neil was appointed Governor of the
Territory and served until 1883.

1881   January 8. Custer County was created,
effective April 1, 1882, with its county
seat at Challis. It was named for Briga-
dier General George Armstrong Custer of
the United States Army who was killed with
all his men at Little Big Horn, Dakota
Territory in June, 1876.

1883   John N. Irwin was appointed Governor of Idaho
Territory and served until 1884.

1884   William M. Bann became Governor of the
Territory and served until 1885.

1885   January 13. Bingham County was established
with its county seat at Blackfoot. It was
named for Henry Harrison Bingham, Civil
War veteran and Representative from Pennsylvania.

September 29. Edward A. Stevenson was
appointed Governor of Idaho Territory.
He served in that capacity until 1889.

1886   The Nez Perce Indians were returned to Idaho
reduced in numbers and suffering from various
illnesses.

1889   January 30. The University of Idaho was
chartered at Moscow, Idaho. The first
classes met in 1892.

February 7. Elmore County was created with
its county seat at Mountain Home. It was
named for Ida Elmore.

George L. Shoup was appointed Governor of the
Territory and served until 1890.

The Constitution of Idaho was adopted as a
preliminary to being admitted as a state.

1890   Population: 88,548.

July 3. Idaho was admitted into the Union
as the 43rd state.

George L. Shoup was elected Governor of the
state and served until his resignation in
December when he became a United States Senator.

December. Norman B. Wiley became Acting
Governor and served until January, 1893.

1891   March 7. Canyon County was established.
            Caldwell was chosen as the county seat.

            The College of Idaho was founded at Caldwell.

1892   October 3. The University of Idaho began
            conducting classes.

            When the Mine Owners' Association began
            discriminating in wages between the miners
            and the surfacemen the union began a strike.
            Violence occurred when non-union men were
            brought in. Eventually Federal troops had
            to be called in to restore order.

1893   January. William J. McConnell, Republican,
            became governor, having been elected in 1892.
            He served until January 4, 1897.

            March 4. Fremont County was established
            with its county seat at St. Anthony. It was
            named for John C. Fremont, third provisional
            governor of California and fifth territorial
            governor of Arizona as well as Senator from
            California.

            March 6. Bannock County was created with
            Pocatello as county seat. It was named for
            the Bannock Indians.

1895   March 5. Blaine County was established with
            its county seat at Hailey. It was named for
            James G. Blaine, Representative and Senator
            from Maine as well as Secretary of State
            under Presidents Garfield and Benjamin Har-
            rison.

            March 18. Lincoln County was created with
            Shoshone as county seat. It was named for
            Abraham Lincoln, 16th President of the United
            States.

1897   January 4. Frank Steunenberg, Democrat and

Populist became Governor, having been elected
in 1896. He served until January 7, 1901.

1900   Population: 161,772.

1901   January 7. Frank W. Hunt, Democratic Popu-
              list became Governor, having been elected in
              1900. He served until January 5, 1903.

1903   January 5. John T. Morrison, Republican,
              who had been elected in 1902, became gover-
              nor and served in office until January 2,
              1905.

1904   Idaho's first federal reclamation project
              was authorized: Minidoka on the Snake River.

1905   January 2. Frank R. Gooding, Republican,
              began serving his term as Governor, contin-
              uing in office for a second term until Janu-
              ary 4, 1909. He was elected in 1904 and
              1906.

              December 30. Former Governor Frank Steunen-
              berg was murdered. The 1907 trial attracted
              international attention.

1907   February 21. Bonner and Twin Falls Counties
              were established. The county seats were
              respectively Sandpoint and Twin Falls. Bon-
              ner County was named for Edwin L. Bonner who
              built and ran a ferry on the Kootenai River
              in 1864.

              Charles H. Haywood, Secretary of the Western
              Federation of Miners was tried on a charge
              of conspiracy in connection with the murder
              of former Governor Frank Steunenberg, but
              he was acquitted.

1909   January 4. James H. Brady, Republican, who
              had been elected in 1908, became Governor of
              Idaho and continued to serve in that office
              until January 2, 1911.

1910   Population: 325,594.

1911   January 2. James H. Hawley, Democrat, became
              Governor of Idaho and served until January 6,
              1913. He had been elected in 1910.

              January 20. The state legislature ratified
              the 16th amendment to the United States

Constitution.

February 7. Bonneville County was established
with its county seat at Idaho Falls. It
was named for Benjamin Louis Eulalie de
Bonneville who served in the United States
Army and also explored the California and
Rocky Mountains area.

March 3. Lewis and Adams Counties were created with their county seats respectively
at Nezperce and Council. Lewis was named for
Meriwether Lewis who had been private secretary to President Thomas Jefferson and led
the expedition with Captain William Clark
which crossed the United States and reached
the Columbia River. Adams County was named
for John Adams, 2nd President of the United
States.

1913   January 6. John M. Haines, Republican, became Governor of the state and served until
January 4, 1915. He had been elected in 1912.

January 20. Franklin County with its county
seat at Preston was founded. It was named
for Franklin Dewey Richards, high priest of
the Church of Latter Day Saints who had led
a group of settlers to Salt Lake Valley in
1848.

January 28. Gooding and Minidoka Counties
were established. Rupert is county seat of
Minidoka and Gooding of Gooding County.
Gooding is named for Frank Robert Gooding,
7th governor of Idaho and Senator from the
state.

January 30. Power County was created with
its county seat at American Falls.

January 31. The state legislature ratified
the 17th Amendment to the United States
Constitution.

February 18. Jefferson and Madison Counties
were established. They were named for Thomas
Jefferson, 3rd President of the United States
and James Madison, 4th President of the United
States. Rigby is the county seat of Jefferson
County and Rexburg of Madison County.

Northwest Nazarene College was founded at Nampa.

1914   January 4. Moses Alexander, Democrat, be-
            came Governor and served in that office un-
            til June 6, 1919. He was elected in 1914 and
            reelected in 1916.

            January 23. Benewah and Boundary Counties
            were created. Benewah with its count seat
            at St. Maries was named for Benewa, a Coeur
            d'Alene Indian Chief, and Boundary with its
            seat at Bonner's Ferry was descriptive for
            the boundary line with Canada.

1915   January 26. Teton County was established and
            named for the Teton Indian Tribe. Its county
            seat is Driggs.

            March 19. Gem County was created with its
            county seat at Emmett.

1917   February 6. Camas County was established;
            a descriptive word for the Camas root. Its
            county seat is Fairfield. Butte County with
            its county seat at Arco was founded.

            February 26. Valley County was founded with
            its seat at Cascade.

            July 16. Payette County, named for Francis
            Payette, was created. Its county seat is
            Payette.

1919   January 6. David W. Davis, Republican, became
            governor and served until January 1, 1923.
            He had been elected in 1918 and was reelected
            in 1920.

            January 8. The state legislature ratified
            the 18th Amendment to the United States Con-
            stitution.

            February 1. Clark County, named for Sam
            Clark, a pioneer cattleman, was created. Its
            county seat is Dubois.

            February 11. Caribou County, named for an
            early settler Caribou Fairchild, was estab-
            lished. Its county seat is Soda Springs.

1920   Population: 431,866.

February 11. The state legislature ratified
the 19th Amendment to the United States Constitution.

1922   The first radio station in the state was es-
            tablished at Boise: KFAV. It is now KIDO.

1923   January 1. Charles C. Moore, Republican,
            became governor. He served until January 3,
            1927, having been elected in 1922 and re-
            elected in 1924.

1927   January 3. H. Clarence Baldridge, Republi-
            can, became governor and served until Janu-
            ary 5, 1931. He had been elected in 1926
            and was reelected in 1928.

1929   Craters of the Moon National Monument was
            established in Idaho.

1930   Population: 445,032

1931   January 5. C. Ben Ross, Democrat, became
            governor, having been elected in 1930. He
            was reelected in 1932 and 1934, serving un-
            til January 4, 1937.

1933   January 21. The state legislature ratified
            the 20th Amendment to the United States Con-
            stitution.

            October 17. The state legislature ratified
            the 21st Amendment to the United States Con-
            stitution.

1936   Sun Valley, a resort, opened.

1937   January 4. Barzilla W. Clark, Democrat, be-
            came Governor, having been elected to the
            office in 1936. He served until January 2,
            1939.

1939   January 2. Clarence A. Bottolfsen, Republican,
            became governor and served until January 6,
            1941. He had been elected in 1938.

1940   Population: 524,873.

1941   January 6. Chase A. Clark, Democrat, became
            governor, having been elected in 1940. He
            served in this office until January 4, 1943.

1943   January 4. Clarence A. Bottolfsen, Republi-

can, again became governor. He had been
elected in 1942 and served until January 1,
1945.

1945   January 9.   Charles C. Gossett, Democrat,
            became governor, having been elected in 1944.
            He resigned on November 17, 1945 to take a
            seat in the United States Senate.

            November 17.   Lieutenant Governor Arnold
            Williams, Democrat, became governor follow-
            ing the resignation of Governor Charles C.
            Gossett. Williams served in the gubernator-
            ial office until the end of the term, January
            6, 1947.

1947   January 6.   Charles A. Robins, Republican,
            became governor. He had been elected in
            1946 and served until January 1, 1951.

1949   The Atomic Energy Commission constructed a
            National Reactor Testing Station near Idaho
            Falls.

1950   Population: 588,637.

1951   January 1.   Len B. Jordan, Republican, be-
            came governor, having been elected to the
            office in 1950. He served until January 3,
            1955.

            January 30.   The state legislature ratified
            the 22nd Amendment to the United States Con-
            stitution.

            December 20.   Electricity was generated from
            atomic energy for the first time at the
            National Reactor Testing Station near Idaho
            Falls.

1953   July.   The state's first television station
            began operating in Boise, KIDO. It is now
            KTVB.

1955   January 3.   Robert E. Smylie, Republican,
            became governor. He had been elected in
            1954 and was reelected in 1958 and 1962,
            serving in the office until January 2, 1967.

            July 17.   Arco became the first community
            to receive its entire power supply from
            atomic energy, beginning with one hour on
            this date.

1959   Engineers completed Brownlee Dam, the first
            of three large hydroelectric dams on the
            Snake River. This project was constructed
            by a private utility company. The entire
            project was completed by 1968.

1960   Population: 667,191

1961   Oxbow Dam, second of the three large hydro-
            electric dams to be constructed on the Snake
            River, was completed.

            January 31. The state legislature ratified
            the 23rd Amendment to the United States Con-
            stitution.

1962   October 8. Oregon, Washington, Wyoming,
            Montana, Nebraska, Utah and Idaho signed
            an interstate pact for development and im-
            provement of the Columbia River.

            The Lewis and Clark Highway was completed
            across the rugged terrain of northern Idaho.

1963   March 8. The state legislature ratified
            the 24th Amendment to the United States
            Constitution.

            September. Despite the June 17 Supreme
            Court ruling banning school prayers the
            public schools in the state continued the
            practice.

1965   Boise State College was founded at Boise,
            and Lewis-Clark State College was founded
            at Lewiston.

            Nez Perce National Historical Park was cre-
            ated. The Dworshak Dam project was started
            on Clearwater River.

1966   March 2. The state legislature ratified
            the 25th Amendment to the United States
            Constitution.

            March 22. Governor Robert E. Smylie signed
            a legislative reapportionment bill which
            was approved by a three-judge federal court
            in April.

1967   January 2. Don Samuelson, Republican, be-
            came governor, having been elected in 1966.
            He served in office until January 4, 1971.

1968   The Hell's Canyon Dam, third of the three
                Snake River private dams was completed.
                It was part of the hydroelectric project
                which provided over one million killowatts
                of power.

                The United States Supreme Court overruled
                the authorization previously given by the
                Federal Power Commission for another power
                dam below the new Hell's Canyon Dam.

1970   Population: 712,567

1971   January 4. Cecil D. Andrus, Democrat, be-
                came governor. He had been elected in 1970.

                March 30. The state legislature ratified the
                26th Amendment to the United States Consti-
                tution.

                April 13. Congressional redistricting was
                enacted as the result of the state's having
                lost one seat in the House of Representatives
                based on the 1970 United States census.

1972   The state legislature ratified the proposed
                Equal Rights Amendment to the United States
                Constitution.

1975   February 15. The largest navigable water
                route in the West was completed and opened.
                This was the Snake River Project, a 469-mile
                water way from Lewiston, Idaho to Astoria,
                Oregon.

1976   June 5. The Teton River Dam burst, killing
                nine persons. At least thirty people were
                missing. Property damage in the Upper Snake
                River Valley totaled approximately $1,000,000.

                July 12. President Gerald R. Ford signed an
                energy bill which contained a rider providing
                approximately $200,000,000 for the victims of
                the Teton Dam disaster.

1977   February 8. The state legislature rescinded
                its ratification of the Equal Rights Amend-
                ment. It had ratified the amendment in
                1972.

BIOGRAPHICAL DIRECTORY

The selected list of governors, United States Senators and members of the House of Representatives for
Idaho, 1890-1977, includes all persons listed in the
Chronology for whom basic biographical data was readily
available. Older biographical sources are frequently
in conflict on certain individuals, and in such cases
the source most commonly cited by later authorities was
preferred.

AINSLEE, George
    Democrat
    b. near Boonville, Mo., October 30, 1838
    d. Oakland, Calif., May 19, 1813
    U. S. Representative (Territorial Delegate), 1879-83

ALEXANDER, Moses
    Democrat
    b. Germany, November 13, 1853
    d. January 4, 1932
    Governor of Idaho, 1915-19

BALDRICH, H. Clarence
    Republican
    b. Carlock, Ill., November 24, 1868
    d. June 7, 1947
    Governor of Idaho, 1927-31

BENNETT, Thomas Warner
    Independent
    b. Union County, Ind., February 16, 1831
    d. Richmond, Ind., February 2, 1893
    Governor of Territory of Idaho, 1871-75
    U. S. Representative (Territorial Delegate), 1875-76

BORAH, William Edgar
    Republican
    b. near Fairfield, Ill., June 29, 1865
    d. Washington, D.C., January 19, 1940
    U. S. Senator, 1907-40

BOTTOLFSEN, Clarence A.
    b. Superior, Wis., October 10, 1891
    d. July 18, 1964
    Governor of Idaho, 1939-41, 1943-45

BRADY, James Henry
    Republican
    b. Indiana County, Pa., June 12, 1862
    d. Washington, D. C., January 13, 1918
    Governor of Idaho, 1909-11
    U. S. Senator, 1913-18

BUDGE, Hamer Harold
    Republican
    b. Pocatello, Ida., November 21, 1910
    U. S. Representative, 1951-61

CHRUCH, Frank Forrester
     Democrat
     b. Boise, Ida., July 25, 1924
     U. S. Senator, 1957-

CLARK, Barzilla W.
     Democrat
     b. Hadley, Ind., December 22, 1881
     d. September 21, 1943
     Governor of Idaho, 1937-39

CLARK, Chase A.
     Democrat
     b. Hadley, Ind., August 21, 1883
     d. December 30, 1966
     Governor of Idaho, 1941-43

CLARK, David Worth
     Democrat
     b. Idaho Falls, Ida., April 2, 1902
     d. Los Angeles, Calif., June 19, 1955
     U. S. Representative, 1935-39
     U. S. Senator, 1939-45

COFFIN, Thomas Chalkley
     Democrat
     b. Caldwell, Ida., October 25, 1887
     d. Washington, D.C.
     U. S. Representative, 1933-34

DAVIS, D. W.
     Republican
     Governor of Idaho, 1919-23

DUBOIS, Fred Thomas
     Democrat
     b. Palestine, Ill., May 29, 1851
     d. Washington, D.C., February 14, 1930
     U. S. Representative (Territorial Delegate), 1887-90
     U. S. Senator, 1891-1907 (Silver Republican, 1901,
          Democrat, 1901-07).

FENN, Stephen Southmyd
     Democrat
     b. Watertown, Conn., March 28, 1820
     d. Blackfoot, Ida., April 13, 1892
     U. S. Representative (Territorial Delegate), 1876-79

FRENCH, Burton Lee
     Republican
     b. near Delph, Ind.
     d. Hamilton, Ohio, September 12, 1954
     U. S. Representative, 1903-09, 1911-15, 1917-32

GLENN, Thomas Louis
    Populist
    b. near Bardwell, Ky., February 2, 1847
    d. Montpelier, Ida., November 18, 1918
    U. S. Representative, 1901-03

GOFF, Abe McGregor
    Republican
    b. Colfax, Wash., December 21, 1899
    U. S. Representative, 1947-49

GOODING, Frank Robert
    Republican
    b. Tiverton, Eng., September 16, 1854
    d. Gooding, Ida., June 24, 1928
    Governor of Idaho, 1905-09
    U. S. Senator, 1921-23

GOSSETT, Charles Clinton
    Democrat
    b. Princeton, Ohio, September 2, 1888
    Governor of Idaho, January-November 16, 1945
    U. S. Senator, 1945-47.

GUNN, James
    Populist
    b. County Fermanagh, Ireland, March 6, 1843
    d. Boise, Ida., November 5, 1911
    U. S. Representative, 1897-99

HAILEY, John
    Democrat
    b. Smith County, Tenn., August 29, 1835
    d. Boise, Ida., April 10, 1921
    U. S. Representative (Territorial Delegate), 1873-75,
        1885-87

HAINES, John M.
    Republican
    b. Jasper County, Ia., January 1, 1863
    d. June 4, 1917
    Governor of Idaho, 1913-15

HAMER, Thomas Ray
    b. Vermont, Ill., May 4, 1864
    d. Phoenix, Ariz., December 22, 1950
    U. S. Representative, 1909-11

HANSEN, George Vernon
    Republican
    b. Tetonia, Ida., September 14, 1930
    U. S. Representative, 1965-69

HANSEN, Orval
    Republican
    b. Firth, Ida., August 3, 1926
    U. S. Representative, 1969-

HARDING, Ralph R.
    Democrat
    b. Malad City, Ida, September 9, 1929
    U. S. Representative, 1961-65

HAWLEY, James H.
    b. Dubuque, Iowa, January 17, 1847
    d. August 3, 1929
    Governor of Idaho, 1911-13

HEITFELD, Henry
    Populist
    b. St. Louis, Mo., January 12, 1859
    d. Spokane, Wash., October 21, 1938
    U. S. Senator, 1897-1903

HEYBURN, Weldon Brinton
    Republican
    b. near Chudds Ford, Pa., May 23, 1852
    d. Washington, D.C., October 17, 1912
    U. S. Senator, 1903-12

HOLBROOK, Edward Dexter
    Democrat
    b. Elyria, Ohio, May 6, 1836
    d. Idaho City, Ida., June 18, 1870
    U. S. Representative (Territorial Delegate), 1865-69

HUNT, Frank W.
    Democrat-Fusionist
    b. Newport, Ky., December 16, 1861
    d. 1906
    Governor of Idaho, 1901-03

JORDAN, Len B.
    Republican
    b. Mount Pleasant, Utah, May 15, 1899
    Governor of Idaho, 1951-55
    U. S. Senator, 1962-

MCCLURE, James Albertus
    Republican
    b. Payette, Ida., December 27, 1924
    U. S. Representative, 1967-

MCCONNELL, William John
    Republican
    b. Commerce, Mich., September 18, 1839

d. Moscow, Ida., March 30, 1925
U. S. Senator, December 18, 1890-91
Governor of Idaho, 1892-96

MCCRACKEN, Robert McDowell
    Republican
    b. Vincennes, Ind., March 5, 1874
    d. Emmett, Ida., May 16, 1934
    U. S. Representative, 1915-17

MERRITT, Samuel Augustus
    Democrat
    b. Staunton, Va., August 15, 1827
    d. Salt Lake City, Utah, September 8, 1910
    U. S. Representative (Territorial Delegate), 1871-73

MILLER, Bert Henry
    Democrat
    b. St. George, Utah, December 15, 1879
    d. Washington, D.C., October 8, 1949
    U. S. Senator 1949

MOORE, Charles C. Moore
    Republican
    b. Holt County, Mo., February 26m 1866
    d. March 19, 1958
    Governor of Idaho, 1923-27.

MORRISON, John T.
    Republican
    b. Jefferson County, Mo., December 25, 1860
    Governor of Idaho, 1903-04

NUGENT, John Frost
    Democrat
    b. La Grande, Oregon, June 28, 1868
    d. Silver Spring, Md., September 19, 1931
    U. S. Senator, 1918-21

PERBY, Kirtland Irving
    Democrat
    b. Smithville, Ohio, February 8, 1867
    d. Los Angeles, Calif., January 9, 1939
    U. S. Senator, 1912-13

PFOST, Gracie Bowers
    Democrat
    b. Harrison, Ark., March 12, 1906
    d. Baltimore, Md., August 11, 1965
    U. S. Representative, 1953-63

POPE, James Pinckney
    b. Jonesboro, La., March 31, 1884
    d. Alexandria, Va., January 23, 1966

U. S. Senator, 1933-39

ROBINS, Charles A.
    Republican
    Governor of Idaho, 1947-51

ROSS, C. Benn
    Democrat
    b. Parma, Ida.
    d. March 31, 1946
    Governor of Idaho, 1931-37

SAMUELSON, Don
    Republican
    Governor of Idaho, 1967-71

SANBORN, John Garfield
    Republican
    b. Chanoa, Ill., September 28, 1885
    d. Boise, Ida., May 16, 1968
    U. S. Representative, 1947-51

SHAFER, Jacob K.
    Democrat
    b. near Broadway, Va., December 26, 1823
    d. Eureka, Nex., November 22, 1876
    U. S. Representative (Territorial Delegate), 1869-71

SHOUP, George Laird
    Republican
    b. Kittanning, Pa., June 15, 1836
    d. Boise, Ida., December 21, 1904
    Territorial Governor of Idaho, 1889-90
    Governor of Idaho, 1890
    U. S. Senator, 1890-1901

SINGISER, Theodore Frelinghuysen
    b. Churchtown, Pa., March 15, 1845
    d. Chicago, Ill., January 23, 1907
    U. S. Representative (Territorial Delegate), 1883-85

SMITH, Addison Taylor
    Representative
    b. Cambridge, Ohio, September 5, 1862
    d. Washington, D.C., July 5, 1956
    U. S. Representative, 1913-33

SMYLIE, Robert E.
    b. Marcus, Iowa, October 31, 1914
    Governor of Idaho, 1955-67

STEUNENBERG, Frank
    Democrat

d. December 30, 1905
Governor of Idaho, 1897-1901

SWEET, Willis
    Republican
    b. Alburg Springs, Vt., January 1, 1856
    d. San Juan, Puerto Rico, July 9, 1925
    U. S. Representative, 1890-95

TAYLOR, Glen Hearst
    Democrat
    b. Portland, Oregon, April 12, 1904
    U. S. Senator, 1945-51

THOMAS, John
    Republican
    b. Phillips County, Kansas, January 4, 1874
    d. Washington, D.C., November 10, 1945
    U. S. Senator, 1928-33, 1940-45

WALLACE, William Henson
    Republican
    b. Troy, Ohio, July 19, 1811
    d. Stelacoom, Wash., February 7, 1879
    U. S. Representative (Territorial Delegate from
        Washington), 1861-63
    Governor of Idaho Territory, 1863
    U. S. Representative, 1864-65

WELKER, Herman
    Republican
    b. Cambridge, Ida., December 11, 1906
    d. Bethesda, Md., October 30, 1957
    U. S. Senator, 1951-57

WHITE, Compton Ignatius
    Democrat
    b. Baton Rouge, La., July 31, 1877.
    d. Spokane, Wash., March 31, 1956
    U. S. Representative, 1933-47, 1949-51

WHITE, Compton Ignatius, Jr.
    Democrat
    b. Spokane, Wash., December 19, 1920
    U. S. Representative, 1963-67

WILLEY, N. B. (Republican)
    b. Guildford, N. Y., March 25, 1838
    d. ----
    Governor of Idaho, 1890-93

    WILLIAMS, Arnold
    Democrat

Governor of Idaho, 1945-47

WILSON, Edgar
    Silver Republican/Democrat
    b. Armstrong County, Pa., February 25, 1861
    d. Boise, Ida., January 3, 1915
    U. S. Representative, 1895-97 (Republican)
        1899-1901 (Silver Republican/Democrat)

WOOD, John Travers
    Republican
    b. Wakefield, England, November 25, 1878
    d. Coeur d'Alene, Ida., November 2, 1954
    U. S. Representative, 1951-53

PROMINENT PERSONALITIES

The following select list of prominent persons of Idaho has been selected to indicate the valuable contributions they have made to American life.

BORGLUM, Gutzon (John Gutzon de la Mothe Borglum)
  b. Idaho, March 25, 1871
  d. March 6, 1941
  Sculptor, painter, author
  Made colossal marble head of Lincoln in the
      rotunda of the Capitol Building, Washing-
      ton, D. C.
  Author and designer of Confederate half dollar
  Designer and sculptor of the first national
      memorial at Black Hills, S. D. - offi-
      cially begun August 10, 1927. Head of
      Washington unveiled, 1930; Jefferson,
      1936; Lincoln, 1937; Theodore Roosevelt,
      1939

BRINK, Carol Ryrie
  b. Moscow Idaho, December 28, 1895
  Author of children's books, beginning 1925
  Books: Caddie Woodlawn, 1935 (Received Newberry
      Medal for year's most distinguished con-
      tribution to juvenile literature)
          The Headland, 1955
          The Twin Cities, 1961
          Louly, 1974

FISHER, Vardis
  b. 1895
  d. 1968
  Author
  Books: Sonnets to an Immaginary Madonna, 1927
          The Neurotic Nightingale, 1935
          Children of God, 1939
          Darkness and the Deep, 1943

HANSBERGER, Robert Vail
  b. Worthington, Minn., June 1, 1920
  Manufacturing company executive
  Director Boise Payette Lumber Co., Idaho,
      1956-57
  President, director, chairman of the board,
      Boise Cascade Corporation, Idaho, 1956-
      72
  Chairman, chief executive officer, chairman
      of the board, Futura Industries Corpora-

                    tion, Boise, Idaho, 1972

JOSEPH
    Indian name: HINMATON-YALAKTIT
    b. 1840?
    d. 1904
    Nez Perce chief
    great strategist in Indian wars, 1877-79
    Defeated and captured by General Nelson A.
        Miles, October 5, 1877

PERRINE, Ira B.
    b. Indiana, 1861
    d. 1947
    Miner, dairyman, and promoter of irrigation
        projects
    Principle leader in development of Magic
        Valley

PIERCE, Elias Davidson
    b. Virginia, 1823
    d. 1897
    Miner - took part in California, British Colum-
        bia and other gold rushes
    Leader of group which discovered gold in
        Idaho
    Pierce City named in his honor

POUND, Ezra Loomis
    b. 1885
    Poet
    Works: Cathay, 1915
           Personae, 1909
           Ripostes, 1912
           Cantos (series of volumes), 1925-49
           Imaginary Letters, 1930
           Guide to Fulchur, 1938

SACAGAWEA (Bird Woman)
    b. 1787
    d. December 20, 1812
    Shoshonean Indian female guide of Lewis and
        Clark Expedition, 1805-06

SPALDING, Henry Harmon
    b. New York, c. 1803
    d. c. 1843
    Missionary who came west with Marcus Whitman in
        1836, brought Christianity and civilization
        to the Nez Perce Indians
    Introduced first agriculture, milling, schools
        and printing known in Idaho

FIRST STATE CONSTITUTION

STATEHOOD PERIOD

The organizing of a separate Montana Territory in 1864, and a separate Wyoming Territory in 1868, enhanced Idaho's prospects for individual statehood candidacy. An enlarged court system was approved in 1867 *(14 Stat. 427),* and a separate Idaho delegate to Congress authorized in 1869 *(15 Stat. 339).* Although territorial laws discriminating against Chinese immigrants were disallowed in 1870 *(16 Stat. 366),* anti-polygamy statutes and attendant disabilities were overlooked or indirectly approved.

A population boom began in the 1880s which promised that the territory would meet this qualification for statehood. From a population of only 39,159 at the beginning of the decade, the census of 1890 would list 142,924 persons. But the prospect of irreconcilable social and economic factions in the Idaho Territory prompted Congress, in 1887-88, to debate the feasibility of dividing the area between Washington and Nevada Territories. The proposal was ultimately defeated, and the beneficial result of the debate was to prompt local movements toward a constitutional convention and early petition for admission as a state.

The constitutional convention which met at Boise City in July 1889, accordingly, was acutely conscious of the religious as well as economic issues to be threshed out by the delegates. The instrument which was agreed upon, when the convention rose on August 6, of necessity embodied a number of novel features which were to provoke some quibbling in Congress before, on July 3, 1890, Idaho was formally admitted as the forty-third state.

Constitution of 1889

Source: 2 Thorpe, *American Charters, Constitutions and Organic Laws,* 918-52

PREAMBLE

[1]   We, the people of the State of Idaho, graceful to Almighty God for our freedom, to secure its blessings and promote our common welfare do establish this Constitution.

ARTICLE I

DECLARATION OF RIGHTS

SECTION 1. All men are by nature free and equal and have certain inalienable rights, among which are enjoying and defending life and liberty, acquiring, possessing, and protecting property, pursuing happiness, and securing safety.

SEC. 2. All political power is inherent in the people. Government is instituted for their equal protection and benefit, and they have the right to alter, reform, or abolish the same whenever they may deem it necessary, and no special privileges or immunities shall ever be granted that may not be altered, revoked, or repealed by the legislature.

SEC. 3. The State of Idaho is an inseparable part of the American Union, and the Constitution of the United States is the supreme law of the land.

SEC. 4. The exercise and enjoyment of religious faith and worship shall forever be guaranteed; and no person shall be denied any civil or political right, privilege, or capacity on account of his religious opinions; but the liberty of conscience hereby secured shall not be construed to dispense with oaths or affirmations, or excuse acts of licentiousness or justify polygamous or other pernicious practices, inconsistent with morality or the peace or safety of the State; nor to permit any person, organization, or association to directly or indirectly aid or abet, counsel or advise, any person to commit the crime of bigamy or polygamy, or any other crime. No person shall be required to attend or support any ministry or place of worship, religious sect or denomination, or pay tithes against his consent; nor shall any preference be given by law to any religious denomination or mode of worship. Bigamy and polygamy are forever prohibited in the State, and the legislature shall provide by law for the punishment of such crimes. [2]

SEC. 5. The privilege of the writ of habeas corpus shall not be suspended unless, in case of rebellion or invasion, the public safety requires it, and then only in such manner as shall be prescribed by law.

SEC. 6. All persons shall be bailable by sufficient sureties, except for capital offenses, where the proof is evident or the presumption great. Excessive bail shall not be required, nor excessive fines imposed, nor cruel and unusual punishments inflicted.

SEC. 7. The right of trial by jury shall remain inviolate; but in civil actions three-fourths of the jury may render a verdict, and the legislature may provide that in all cases of misdemeanors five-sixths of the jury may render a verdict. A trial by jury may be waived in all criminal cases not amounting to felony by the consent of both parties, expressed in open court, and in civil actions by the consent of the parties, signified in such manner as may be prescribed by law. In civil actions and cases of misdemeanor the jury may consist of twelve, or of any number less than twelve upon which the parties may agree in open court. [3]

SEC. 8. No person shall be held to answer for any felony or criminal offense of any grade, unless on presentment or indictment of a grand jury or on information of the public prosecutor, after a commitment by a magistrate, except in cases of impeachment, in cases cognizable by probate courts or by justices of the peace, and in cases arising in the militia when in actual service in time of war or public danger: *Provided*, That a grand jury may be summoned upon the order of the district court in the manner provided by law: *And provided further*, That after a charge has been ignored by a grand jury, no person shall be held to answer or for trial therefor upon information of the public prosecutor.

SEC. 9. Every person may freely speak, write, and publish on all subjects, being responsible for the abuse of that liberty.

SEC. 10. The people shall have the right to assemble in a peaceable manner to consult for their common good; to instruct their representatives, and to petition the Legislature for the redress of grievances.

SEC. 11. The people have the right to bear arms for their security and defense; but the Legislature shall regulate the exercise of this right by law.

SEC. 12. The military shall be subordinate to the civil power; and no soldier in time of peace shall be quartered in any house without the consent of its owner, nor in time of war except in the manner prescribed by law.

SEC. 13. In all criminal prosecutions, the party accused shall have the right to a speedy and public trial; to have the process of the court to compel the attendance of witnesses in his behalf, and to appear and defend in person and with counsel.

No person shall be twice put in jeopardy for the same offense; nor be compelled in any criminal case to be a witness against himself, nor be deprived of life, liberty or property without due process of law.

SEC. 14. The necessary use of lands for the construction of reservoirs or storage basins, for the purposes of irrigation, or for rights of way for the construction of canals, ditches, flumes, or pipes, to convey water to the place of use, for any useful, beneficial, or necessary purpose, or for drainage; or for the drainage of mines, or the working thereof, by means of roads, railroads, tramways, cuts, tunnels, shafts, hoisting works, dumps, or other necessary means to their complete development, or any other use necessary to the complete development of the material resources of the State, or the preservation of the health of its inhabitants, is hereby declared to be a public use, and
[4]   subject to the regulation and control of the State.

Private property may be taken for public use, but not until a just compensation, to be ascertained in a manner prescribed by law, shall be paid therefor.

SEC. 15. There shall be no imprisonment for debt in this State except in cases of fraud.

SEC. 16. No bill of attainder, ex post facto law, or law impairing the obligation of contracts, shall ever be passed.

SEC. 17. The right of the people to be secure in their persons, houses, papers and effects against unreasonable searches and seizures shall not be violated; and no warrant shall issue without probable cause, shown by affidavit, particularly describing the place to be searched and the person or thing to be seized.

SEC. 18. Courts of justice shall be open to every person, and a speedy remedy afforded for every injury of person, property or character, and right and justice shall be administered without sale, denial, delay, or prejudice.

SEC. 19. No power, civil or military, shall at any time interfere with or prevent the free and lawful exercise of the right of suffrage.

SEC. 20. No property qualification shall ever be required for any person to vote or hold office except in school elections or elections
[5]   creating indebtedness.

SEC. 21. This enumeration of rights shall not be construed to impair or deny other rights retained by the people.

ARTICLE II

DISTRIBUTION OF POWERS

SECTION 1. The powers of the government of this State are divided into three distinct departments, the Legislative, Executive

and Judicial; and no person or collection of persons charged with
the exercise of powers properly belonging to one of these departments,
shall exercise any powers properly belonging to either of the others,
except as in this Constitution expressly directed or permitted.

ARTICLE III

LEGISLATIVE DEPARTMENT

SECTION 1. The legislative power of the State shall be vested in
a senate and house of representatives. The enacting clause of every
bill shall be as follows: " Be it enacted by the Legislature of the
State of Idaho."

SEC. 2. The senate shall consist of eighteen members and the house
of representatives of thirty-six members. The Legislature may
increase the number of senators and representatives: *Provided*, The
number of senators shall never exceed twenty-four, and the house of
representatives shall never exceed sixty members. The senators
and representatives shall be chosen by the electors of the respective
counties or districts into which the State may from time to time be
divided by law.

SEC. 3. The senators and representatives shall be elected for the
term of two years, from and after the first day of December next
following the general election.

SEC. 4. The members of the first legislature shall be apportioned
to the several legislative districts of the State in proportion to the
number of votes polled at the last general election for Delegate to
Congress, and thereafter to be apportioned as may be provided by
law: *Provided*, Each county shall be entitled to one representative.

SEC. 5. A senatorial or representative district, when more than
one county shall constitute the same, shall be composed of contiguous
counties and no county shall be divided in creating such districts.

SEC. 6. No person shall be a senator or representative who at the
time of his election is not a citizen of the United States and an elector
of this State, nor any one who has not been for one year next preceding his election an elector of the county or district whence he may
be chosen.

SEC. 7. Senators and representatives, in all cases except for treason,
felony, or breach of the peace, shall be privileged from arrest during
the session of the Legislature, and in going to and returning from the
same, and shall not be liable to any civil process during the session
of the Legislature, nor during the ten days next before the commencement thereof; nor shall a member for words uttered in debate in
either house be questioned in any other place.

SEC. 8. The sessions of the Legislature shall, after the first session
thereof, be held biennially, at the Capital of the State, commencing
on the first Monday after the first day of January, and every second
year thereafter, unless a different day shall have been appointed by
law, and at other times when convened by the Governor.

SEC. 9. Each house when assembled shall choose its own officers,
judge of the election, qualifications, and returns of its own members,
determine its own rules of proceeding, and sit upon its own adjourn-
ments; but neither house shall, without the concurrence of the other,

adjourn for more than three days, nor to any other place than that in which it may be sitting.

SEC. 10. A majority of each house shall constitute a quorum to do business, but a smaller number may adjourn from day to day, and may compel the attendance of absent members in such manner and under such penalties as such house may provide. A quorum being in attendance, if either house fail to effect an organization within the first four days thereafter, the members of the house so failing shall be entitled to no compensation from the end of the said four days until an organization shall have been effected.

SEC. 11. Each house may, for good cause shown, with the concurrence of two-thirds of all the members, expel a member.

SEC. 12. The business of each house, and of the committee of the whole, shall be transacted openly and not in secret session.

SEC. 13. Each house shall keep a journal of its proceedings; and the yeas and nays of the members of either house an any question, shall, at the request of any three members present, be entered on the journal.

SEC. 14. Bills may originate in either house, but may be amended or rejected in the other, except that bills for raising revenue shall originate in the house of representatives.

SEC. 15. No law shall be passed except by bill, nor shall any bill be put upon its final passage until the same, with the amendments thereto, shall have been printed for the use of the members; nor shall any bill become a law unless the same shall have been read on three several days in each house previous to the final vote thereon: *Provided*, In case of urgency, two-thirds of the house where such bill may be pending may, upon a vote of the yeas and nays, dispense with this provision. On the final passage of all bills they shall be read at length, section by section, and the vote shall be by yeas and nays upon each bill separately, and shall be entered upon the journal; and no bill shall become a law without the concurrence of a majority of the members present.

SEC. 16. Every act shall embrace but one subject and matters properly connected therewith, which subject shall be expressed in the title; but if any subject shall be embraced in an act which shall not be expressed in the title, such act shall be void only as to so much thereof as shall not be embraced in the title.

SEC. 17. Every act or joint resolution shall be plainly worded, avoiding as far as practicable the use of technical terms.

SEC. 18. No act shall be revised or amended by mere reference to its title, but the section as amended shall be set forth and published at full length.

SEC. 19. The legislature shall not pass local or special laws in any of the following enumerated cases, that is to say:

Regulating the jurisdiction and duties of justices of the peace and constables.

For the punishment of crimes and misdemeanors.

Regulating the practice of the courts of justice.

Providing for a change of venue in civil or criminal actions.

Granting divorces.

Changing the names of persons or places.

Authorizing the laying out, opening, altering, maintaining, working on, or vacating roads, highways, streets, alleys, town plats, parks, cemeteries, or any public grounds not owned by the State.

Summoning and impanneling grand and trial juries, and providing for their compensation.

Regulating county and township business, or the election of county and township officers.

For the assessment and collection of taxes.

Providing for and conducting elections, or designating the place of voting.

Affecting estates of deceased persons, minors, or other persons under legal disabilities.

Extending the time for collection of taxes.

Giving effect to invalid deeds, leases or other instruments.

Refunding money paid into the State treasury.

Releasing or extinguishing, in whole or in part, the indebtedness, liability or obligation of any person or corporation in this State, or any municipal corporation therein.

Declaring any person of age, or authorizing any minor to sell, lease, or encumber his or her property.

Legalizing as against the State the unauthorized or invalid act of any officer.

Exempting property from taxation.

Changing county seats; unless the law authorizing the change shall require that two-thirds of the legal votes cast at a general or special election shall designate the place to which the county seat shall be changed: *Provided*, That the power to pass a special law shall cease as long as the legislature shall provide for such change by general law: *Provided further*, That no special law shall be passed for any one county oftener than once in six years.

Restoring to citizenship persons convicted of infamous crimes.

Regulating the interest on money.

Authorizing the creation, extension or impairing of liens.

Chartering or licensing ferries, bridges or roads.

Remitting fines, penalties or forfeitures.

Providing for the management of common schools.

Creating offices or prescribing the powers and duties of officers in counties, cities, townships, election districts, or school districts, except as in this Constitution otherwise provided.

Changing the law of descent or succession.

Authorizing the adoption or legitimization of children.

For limitation of civil or criminal actions.

Creating any corporation.

Creating, increasing or decreasing fees, percentages, or allowances of public officers during the term for which said officers are elected or appointed.

SEC. 20. The Legislature shall not authorize any lottery or gift enterprise under any pretense or for any purpose whatever.

SEC. 21. All bills or joint resolutions passed shall be signed by the presiding officers of the respective houses.

SEC. 22. No act shall take effect until sixty days from the end of the session at which the same shall have been passed, except in case

of emergency, which emergency shall be declared in the preamble or
in the body of the law.

SEC. 23. Each member of the Legislature shall receive for his
services a sum not exceeding five dollars per day from the commencement of the session, but such pay shall not exceed for each member,
except the presiding officers, in the aggregate three hundred dollars
for per diem allowances for any one session; and shall receive each
the sum of ten cents per mile each way by the usual traveled route.

When convened in extra session by the Governor, they shall each
receive five dollars per day; but no extra session shall continue for
a longer period than twenty days, except in case of the first session
of the Legislature. They shall receive such mileage as is allowed
for regular sessions. The presiding officers of the Legislature shall
each in virtue of his office receive an additional compensation equal
to one-half his per diem allowance as a member: *Provided*, That
whenever any member of the Legislature shall travel on a free pass
in coming to or returning from the session of the Legislature, the
number of miles actually traveled on such pass shall be deducted
from the mileage of such member.

SEC. 24. The first concern of all good government is the virtue
and sobriety of the people, and the purity of the home. The Legislature should further all wise and well directed efforts for the promo-
tion of temperance and morality.

SEC. 25. The members of the Legislature shall, before they enter
upon the duties of their respective offices, take or subscribe the following oath or affirmation: " I do solemnly swear (or affirm, as the
case may be) that I will support the Constitution of the United States
and the Constitution of the State of Idaho, and that I will faithfully
discharge the duties of senator (or representative, as the case may be)
according to the best of my ability." And such oath may be administered by the Governor, Secretary of State, or judge of the supreme
court, or presiding officer of either house.

ARTICLE IV

EXECUTIVE DEPARTMENT

SECTION 1. The executive department shall consist of a Governor,
Lieutenant-Governor, Secretary of State, State Auditor, State Treasurer, Attorney-General, and Superintendent of Public Instruction,
each of whom shall hold his office for two years beginning on the first
Monday in January next after his election, except as otherwise provided in this Constitution. The officers of the executive department,
excepting the Lieutenant-Governor, shall, during their terms of office,
reside at the seat of government, where they shall keep the public
records, books, and papers. They shall perform such duties as are
prescribed by this Constitution and as may be prescribed by law.

SEC. 2. The officers named in section one of this article shall be
elected by the qualified electors of the State at the time and places of
voting for members of the Legislature, and the persons, respectively,
having the highest number of votes for the office voted for shall be
elected; but if two or more shall have an equal and the highest number of votes for any one of said offices, the two houses of the Legislature at its next regular session, shall forthwith, by joint ballot, elect

one of such persons for said office. The returns of election for the officers named in section one shall be made in such manner as may be prescribed by law, and all contested elections of the same, other than provided for in this section, shall be determined as may be prescribed by law.

SEC. 3. No person shall be eligible to the office of Governor or Lieutenant-Governor unless he shall have attained the age of thirty years at the time of his election; nor to the office of Secretary of State, State Auditor, Superintendent of Public Instruction, or State Treasurer unless he shall have attained the age of twenty-five years; nor to the office of Attorney-General unless he shall have attained the age of thirty years, and have been admitted to practice in the supreme court of the State or Territory of Idaho, and be in good standing at the time of his election. In addition to the qualifications above described each of the officers named shall be a citizen of the United States and shall have resided within the State or Territory two years next preceding his election.

SEC. 4. The Governor shall be commander-in-chief of the military forces of the State, except when they shall be called into actual service of the United States. He shall have power to call out the militia to execute the laws, to suppress insurrection, or to repel invasion.

SEC. 5. The supreme executive power of the State is vested in the Governor, who shall see that the laws are faithfully executed.

SEC. 6. The Governor shall nominate and, by and with the consent of the senate, appoint all officers whose offices are established by this Constitution, or which may be created by law and whose appointment or election is not otherwise provided for. If, during the recess of the senate, a vacancy occurs in any State or district office, the Governor shall appoint some fit person to discharge the duties thereof until the next meeting of the senate, when he shall nominate some person to fill such office. If the office of a Justice of the supreme or district court, Secretary of State, State Auditor, State Treasurer, Attorney-General, or Superintendent of Public Instruction shall be vacated by death, resignation or otherwise, it shall be the duty of the Governor to fill the same by appointment, and the appointee shall hold his office until his successor shall be elected and qualified in such manner as may be provided by law.

SEC. 7. The Governor, Secretary of State, and Attorney-General shall constitute a board to be known as the board of pardons. Said board, or a majority thereof, shall have power to remit fines and forfeitures, and to grant commutations and pardons after conviction and judgment, either absolutely or upon such conditions as they may impose, in all cases of offenses against the State except treason or conviction on impeachment. The Legislature shall by law prescribe the sessions of said board and the manner in which applications shall be made and regulate the proceedings thereon; but no fine or forfeiture shall be remitted, and no commutation or pardon granted, except by the decision of a majority of said board, after a full hearing in open session, and until previous notice of the time and place of such hearing and the release applied for shall have been given by publication in some newspaper of general circulation at least once a week for four weeks. The proceedings and decision of the board shall be reduced to writing and with their reasons for their action in each case, and the dissent of any member who may disagree, signed by him, and filed, with all papers used upon the hearing, in the office of the Secretary of State.

The Governor shall have power to grant respites or reprieves in all cases of convictions for offenses against the State, except treason or conviction on impeachment, but such respites or reprieves shall not extend beyond the next session of the board of pardons; and such board shall at such session continue or determine such respite or reprieve, or they may commute or pardon the offense, as herein provided. In cases of conviction for treason the governor shall have the power to suspend the execution of the sentence until the case shall be reported to the Legislature at its next regular session, when the Legislature shall either pardon or commute the sentence, direct its execution, or grant a further reprieve. He shall communicate to the Legislature, at each regular session, each case of remission of fine or forfeitue, reprieve, commutation, or pardon granted since the last previous report, stating the name of the convict, the crime of which he was convicted, the sentence and its date, and the date of remission, commutation, pardon, or reprieve, with the reasons for granting the same, and the objections, if any, of any member of the board made thereto.

SEC. 8. The Governor may require information in writing from the officers of the executive department upon any subject relating to the duties of their respective offices, which information shall be given upon oath whenever so required; he may also require information in writing, at any time, under oath, from all officers and managers of State institutions, upon any subject relating to the condition, management and expenses of their respective offices and institutions, and may at any time he deems it necessary, appoint a committee to investigate and report to him upon the condition of any executive office or State institution. The Governor shall at the commencement of each session, and from time to time, by message, give to the Legislature information of the condition of the State, and shall recommend such measures as he shall deem expedient. He shall also send to the Legislature a statement, with vouchers, of the expenditures of all moneys belonging to the State and paid out by him. He shall also, at the commencement of each session, present estimates of the amount of money required to be raised by taxation for all purposes of the State.

SEC. 9. The Governor may, on extraordinary occasions, convene the Legislature by proclamation, stating the purposes for which he has convened it; but when so convened it shall have no power to legislate on any subjects other than those specified in the proclamation; but may provide for the expenses of the session and other matters incidental thereto. He may also, by proclamation, convene the Senate in extraordinary session for the transaction of executive business.

SEC. 10. Every bill passed by the Legislature shall, before it becomes a law, be presented to the Governor. If he approve, he shall sign it, and thereupon it shall become a law; but if he do not approve, he shall return it with his objections to the House in which it originated, which House shall enter the objections at large upon its journals and proceed to reconsider the bill. If then two-thirds of the members present agree to pass the same it shall be sent, together with the objections, to the other House, by which it shall likewise be reconsidered; and if approved by two-thirds of the members present in that House, it shall become a law, notwithstanding the objections of the Governor. In all such cases the vote of each House shall be determined by yeas and nays, to be entered on the journal. Any bill which shall not be returned by the Governor to the Legislature within five days, (Sundays excepted) after it shall have been presented to him, shall become a law in like manner, as if he had signed it, unless the Legislature shall, by adjournment, prevent its return, in which case it shall be filed, with his objections, in the office of the Secretary of State within ten days after such adjournment (Sundays excepted) or become a law.

SEC. 11. The Governor shall have power to disapprove of any item or items of any bill making appropriations of money embracing distinct items, and the part or parts approved shall become a law and the item or items disapproved shall be void, unless enacted in the manner following: If the Legislature be in session, he shall within five days transmit to the House within which the bill originated a copy of the item or items thereof disapproved, together with his objections thereto, and the items objected to shall be separately reconsidered, and each item shall then take the same course as is prescribed for the passage of bills over the executive veto.

SEC. 12. In case of the failure to qualify, the impeachment, or conviction of treason, felony, or other infamous crime of the Governor, or his death, removal from office, resignation, absence from the State, or inability to discharge the powers and duties of his office, the powers, duties and emoluments of the office for the residue of the term, or until the disability shall cease, shall devolve upon the Lieutenant-Governor.

SEC. 13. The Lieutenant-Governor shall be President of the Senate, but shall vote only when the Senate is equally divided. In case of the absence or disqualification of the Lieutenant-Governor from any cause which applies to the Governor, or when he shall hold the office of Governor, then the president pro tempore of the Senate shall perform the duties of the Lieutenant-Governor until the vacancy is filled or the disability removed.

SEC. 14. In case of the failure to qualify in his office, death, resignation, absence from the State, impeachment, conviction of treason, felony or other infamous crime, or disqualification from any cause, of both Governor and Lieutenant-Governor, the duties of the Governor shall devolve upon the president of the Senate pro tempore, until such disqualification of either the Governor or Lieutenant-Governor be removed, or the vacancy filled; and if the president of the Senate, for any of the above named causes, shall become incapable of performing the duties of Governor, the same shall devolve upon the speaker of the House.

SEC. 15. There shall be a seal of this State, which shall be kept by the Secretary of State and used by him officially, and shall be called " The great seal of the State of Idaho." The seal of the Territory of Idaho, as now used, shall be the seal of the State until otherwise provided by law.

SEC. 16. All grants and permissions shall be in the name and by the authority of the State of Idaho, sealed with the great seal of the State, signed by the Governor, and countersigned by the Secretary of State.

Sec. 17. An account shall be kept by the officers of the executive department and of all public institutions of the State of all moneys received by them severally, from all sources, and for every service performed, and of all moneys disbursed by them severally, and a semi-annual report thereof shall be made to the Governor, under oath; they shall also, at least twenty days preceding each regular session, of the Legislature, make full and complete reports of their official transactions to the Governor, who shall transmit the same to the Legislature.

Sec. 18. The Governor, Secretary of State, and Attorney-General shall constitute a board of State prison commissioners, which board shall have such supervision of all matters connected with the State prison as may be prescribed by law. They shall also constitute a board of examiners, with power to examine all claims against the State, except salaries or compensation of officers fixed by law, and perform such other duties as may be prescribed by law. And no claim against the State, except salaries and compensation of officers fixed by law, shall be passed upon by the Legislature without first having been considered and acted upon by said board.

Sec. 19. The Governor, Secretary of State, State Auditor, State Treasurer, Attorney-General, and Superintendent of Public Instruction shall, quarterly as due, during their continuance in office, receive for their services compensation, which for the term next ensuing after the adoption of this Constitution, is fixed as follows: Governor, three thousand dollars per annum; Secretary of State, one thousand eight hundred dollars per annum; State Auditor, one thousand eight hundred dollars per annum; State Treasurer, one thousand dollars per annum; Attorney-General, two thousand dollars per annum; and Superintendent of Public Instruction, one thousand five hundred dollars per annum. The Lieutenant-Governor shall receive the same per diem as may be provided by law for the speaker of the House of Representatives, to be allowed only during the session of the Legislature. The compensations enumerated shall be in full for all services by said officers respectively, rendered in any official capacity or employment whatever during their respective terms of office.

No officer named in this section shall receive for the performance of any official duty any fee for his own use, but all fees fixed by law for the performance by either of them of any official duty shall be collected in advance and deposited with the State Treasurer quarterly to the credit of the State. The Legislature may, by law, diminish or increase the compensation of any or all of the officers named in this section, but no such diminution or increase shall affect the salaries of the officers then in office during their term. *Provided, however,* The Legislature may provide for the payment of actual and necessary expenses to the Governor, Lieutenant-Governor, Secretary of State, Attorney-General, and Superintendent of Public Instruction, while traveling within the State in the performance of official duty.

ARTICLE V

JUDICIAL DEPARTMENT

Section 1. The distinctions between actions at law and suits in equity, and the forms of all such actions and suits, are hereby prohibited; and there shall be in this State but one form of action for the enforcement or protection of private rights or the redress of private wrongs, which shall be denominated a civil action; and every action prosecuted by the people of the State as a party against a person charged with a public offense for the punishment of the same, shall be termed a criminal action.

Feigned issues are prohibited, and the fact at issue shall be tried by order of court before a jury.

SEC. 2. The judicial power of the State shall be vested in a court for the trial of impeachments, a supreme court, district courts, probate courts, courts of justices of the peace, and such other courts inferior to the supreme court as may be established by law for any incorporated city or town.

SEC. 3. The court for the trial of impeachments shall be the senate. A majority of the members elected shall be necessary to a quorum, and the judgment shall not extend beyond removal from, and disqualification to hold office in this State; but the party shall be liable to indictment and punishment according to law.

SEC. 4. The house of representatives solely shall have the power of impeachment. No person shall be convicted without the concurrence of two-thirds of the senators elected. When the Governor is impeached the Chief Justice shall preside.

SEC. 5. Treason against the State shall consist only in levying war against it, or adhering to its enemies, giving them aid and comfort. No person shall be convicted of treason unless on the testimony of two witnesses to the same overt act, or on confession in open court. No conviction of treason or attainder shall work corruption of blood or forfeiture of estate.

SEC. 6. The supreme court shall consist of three Justices, a majority of whom shall be necessary to make a quorum or pronounce a decision. The Justices of the supreme court shall be elected by the electors of the State at large. The terms of office of the justices of the supreme court, except as in this article otherwise provided, shall be six years. The Justices of the supreme court shall, immediately after the first election under this Constitution, be selected by lot, so that one shall hold his office for the term of two years, one for the term of four years, and one for the term of six years. The lots shall be drawn by the Justices of the supreme court, who shall, for that purpose, assemble at the seat of government, and they shall cause the result thereof to be certified to by the Secretary of State and filed in his office. The Justice having the shortest term to serve, not holding his office by appointment or election to fill a vacancy, shall be the Chief Justice, and shall preside at all terms of the supreme court, and, in case of his absence, the Justice having in like manner the next shortest term to serve shall preside in his stead.

SEC. 7. No Justice of the supreme court shall be eligible to any other office of trust or profit under the laws of this State during the term for which he was elected.

SEC. 8. At least four terms of the supreme court shall be held annually; two terms at the seat of State government, and two terms at the city of Lewiston, in Nez Perce County. In case of epidemic, pestilence, or destruction of court houses, the Justices may hold the terms of the supreme court provided by this section at other convenient places, to be fixed by a majority of said Justices. After six years the Legislature may alter the provisions of this section.

Sec. 9. The supreme court shall have jurisdiction to review, upon appeal, any decision of the district courts, or the judges thereof. The supreme court shall also have original jurisdiction to issue writs of mandamus, certiorari, prohibition, and habeas corpus, and all writs necessary or proper to the complete exercise of its appellate jurisdiction.

Sec. 10. The supreme court shall have original jurisdiction to hear claims against the State, but its decision shall be merely recommendatory; no process in the nature of execution shall issue thereon; they shall be reported to the next session of the Legislature for its action.

Sec. 11. The State shall be divided into five judicial districts, for each of which a judge shall be chosen by the qualified electors thereof, whose term of office shall be four years. And there shall be held a district court in each county, at least twice in each year, to continue for such time in each county as may be prescribed by law; but the Legislature may reduce or increase the number of districts, district judges, and district attorneys. This section shall not be construed to prevent the holding of special terms under such regulations as may be provided by law.

Sec. 12. Every judge of the district court shall reside in the district for which he is elected. A judge of any district court may hold a district court in any county at the request of the judge of the district court thereof, and upon the request of the Governor it shall be his duty to do so; but a cause in the district court may be tried by a judge pro tempore, who must be a member of the bar, agreed upon in writing by the parties litigant, or their attorneys of record, and sworn to try the cause.

Sec. 13. The Legislature shall have no power to deprive the judicial department of any power or jurisdiction which rightfully pertains to it as a co-ordinate department of the government; but the Legislature shall provide a proper system of appeals, and regulate by law, when necessary, the methods of proceeding in the exercise of their powers of all the courts below the supreme court, so far as the same may be done without conflict with this Constitution.

Sec. 14. The Legislature may provide for the establishment of special courts for the trial of misdemeanors in incorporated cities and towns where the same may be necessary.

Sec. 15. The clerk of the supreme court shall be appointed by the court, and shall hold his office during the pleasure of the court. He shall receive such compensation for his services as may be provided by law.

Sec. 16. A clerk of the district court for each county shall be elected by the qualified voters thereof at the time and in the manner prescribed by law for the election of members of the Legislature, and shall hold his office for the term of four years.

Sec. 17. The salary of the Justices of the supreme court, until otherwise provided by the Legislature, shall be three thousand dollars each per annum, and the salary of the judges of the district court, until otherwise provided by the Legislature, shall be three thousand dollars each per annum, and no Justice of the supreme court, or judge of the district court, shall be paid his salary, or any part thereof, unless he shall have first taken and subscribed an oath that there is not in his hands any matter in controversy not decided by him which had been finally submitted for his consideration and determination, thirty days prior to the taking and subscribing such oath.

SEC. 18. A district attorney shall be elected, for each judicial district by the qualified electors thereof, who shall hold office for the term of four years, and perform such duties as may be prescribed by law. He shall be a practicing attorney at law and a resident and elector of the district. He shall receive as compensation for his services twenty-five hundred dollars per annum.

SEC. 19. All vacancies occurring in the offices provided for by this article of the Constitution shall be filled as provided by law.

SEC. 20. The district court shall have original jurisdiction in all cases, both at law and in equity, and such appellate jurisdiction as may be conferred by law.

SEC. 21. The probate courts shall be courts of record, and shall have original jurisdiction in all matters of probate, settlement of estates of deceased persons, and appointment of guardians; also jurisdiction to hear and determine all civil cases wherein the debt or damage claimed does not exceed the sum of five hundred dollars, exclusive of interest, and concurrent jurisdiction with justices of the peace in criminal cases.

SEC. 22. In each county of this State there shall be elected justices of the peace as prescribed by law. Justices of the peace shall have such jurisdiction as may be conferred by law, but they shall not have jurisdiction of any cause wherein the value of the property or the amount in controversy exceeds the sum of three hundred dollars, exclusive of interest, nor where the boundaries or title to any real property shall be called in question.

SEC. 23. No person shall be eligible to the office of district judge unless he be learned in the law, thirty years of age, and a citizen of the United States, and shall have resided in the State or Territory at least two years next preceeding his election, nor unless he shall have been at the time of his election, an elector in the judicial district for which he is elected.

SEC. 24. Until otherwise provided by law, the judicial districts shall be five in number, and constituted of the following counties, viz: First district, Shoshone and Kootenai; second district, Latah, Nez Perce. and Idaho; third district, Washington, Ada, Boise, and Owyhee: fourth district, Cassia, Elmore, Logan, and Alturas; fifth district, Bear Lake, Bingham, Oneida, Lemhi, and Custer.

SEC. 25. The judges of the district courts shall, on or before the first day of July in each year, report in writing to the Justices of the supreme court, such defects or omissions in the laws as their knowledge and experience may suggest, and the Justices of the supreme court shall, on or before the first day of December of each year, report in writing to the Governor, to be by him transmitted to the Legislature, together with his message, such defects and omissions in the Constitution and laws as they may find to exist.

SEC. 26. All laws relating to courts shall be general and of uniform operation throughout the State, and the organized judicial powers, proceedings, and practices of all the courts of the same class or grade, so far as regulated by law, and the force and effect of the proceedings, judgments, and decrees of such courts, severally, shall be uniform.

SEC. 27. The Legislature may by law diminish or increase the compensation of any or all the following officers, to-wit: Governor, Lieutenant-Governor, Secretary of State, State Auditor, State Treasurer, Attorney-General, Superintendent of Public Instruction, commissioner of immigration and labor, Justices of the Supreme Court, and judges of the district courts and district attorneys; but no diminution or increase shall affect the compensation of the officer then in office during his term: *Provided, however,* That the Legislature may provide for the payment of actual and necessary expenses of the Governor, Secretary of State, Attorney-General, and Superintendent of Public Instruction incurred while in performance of official duty.

ARTICLE VI

SUFFRAGE AND ELECTIONS

SECTION 1. All elections by the people must be by ballot. An absolutely secret ballot is hereby guaranteed, and it shall be the duty of the Legislature to enact such laws as shall carry this section into effect.

SEC. 2. Except as in this article otherwise provided, every male citizen of the United States, twenty-one years old, who has actually resided in this State or Territory for six months, and in the county where he offers to vote, thirty days next preceding the day of election, if registered as provided by law, is a qualified elector; and until otherwise provided by the Legislature, women who have the qualifications prescribed in this article, may continue to hold such school offices and vote at such school elections as provided by the laws of [6]   Idaho Territory.

SEC. 3. No person is permitted to vote, serve as a juror, or hold any civil office who is under guardianship, idiotic or insane, or who has, at any place, been convicted of treason, felony, embezzlement of the public funds, bartering or selling, or offering to barter or sell his vote, or purchasing or offering to purchase the vote of another, or other infamous crime, and who has not been restored to the rights of citizenship, or who, at the time of such election, is confined in prison on conviction of a criminal offense, or who is a bigamist or polygamist, or is living in what is known as patriarchal, plural or celestial marriage, or in violation of any law of this State, or of the United States, forbidding any such crime; or who, in any manner, teaches, advises, counsels, aids, or encourages any person to enter into bigamy, polygamy, or such patriarchal, plural, or celestial marriage, or to live in violation of any such law, or to commit any such crime; or who is a member of or contributes to the support, aid, or encouragement of any order, organization, association, corporation or society, which teaches, advises, counsels, encourages, or aids any person to enter into bigamy, polygamy or such patriarchal, or plural marriage, or which teaches or advises that the laws of this State prescribing rules of civil conduct, are not the supreme law of the State; nor shall Chinese, or persons of Mongolian descent, not born in the United States, nor Indians not taxed, who have not severed their tribal relations and adopted the habits of civilization, either vote, serve as jurors, or hold any civil office.

SEC. 4. The Legislature may prescribe qualifications, limitations, and conditions for the right of suffrage additional to those prescribed in this article, but shall never annul any of the provisions in this article contained.

SEC. 5. For the purpose of voting, no person shall be deemed to have gained or lost a residence by reason of his presence or absence while employed in the service of this State, or of the United States, nor while engaged in the navigation of the waters of this State or of the United States, nor while a student of any institution of learning, nor while kept at any alms-house or other asylum at the public expense.

ARTICLE VII

FINANCE AND REVENUE

SECTION 1. The fiscal year shall commence on the second Monday of January in each year, unless otherwise provided by law.

SEC. 2. The Legislature shall provide such revenue as may be needful, by levying a tax by valuation, so that every person or corporation shall pay a tax in proportion to the value of his, her, or its property, except as in this article hereinafter otherwise provided. The Legislature may also impose a license tax (both upon natural persons and upon corporations, other than municipal, doing business in this State); also a per capita tax: *Provided*, The legislature may exempt a limited amount of improvements upon land from taxation.

SEC. 3. The word "property" as herein used shall be defined and classified by law.

SEC. 4. The property of the United States, the State, counties, towns, cities, and other municipal corporations and public libraries, shall be exempt from taxation.

SEC. 5. All taxes shall be uniform upon the same class of subjects within the territorial limits, of the authority levying the tax, and shall be levied and collected under general laws, which shall prescribe such regulations as shall secure a just valuation for taxation of all property, real and personal: *Provided*, That the Legislature may allow such exemptions from taxation from time to time as shall seem necessary and just, and all existing exemptions provided by the laws of the Territory, shall continue until changed by the Legislature of the State: *Provided further*, That duplicate taxation of property for the same purpose during the same year, is hereby prohibited.

SEC. 6. The Legislature shall not impose taxes for the purpose of any county, city, town, or other municipal corporation, but may by law invest in the corporate authorities thereof, respectively, the power to assess and collect taxes for all purposes of such corporation.

SEC. 7. All taxes levied for State purposes shall be paid into the State Treasury, and no county, city, town, or other municipal corporation, the inhabitants thereof, nor the property therein, shall be released or discharged from their or its proportionate share of taxes to be levied for State purposes.

SEC. 8. The power to tax corporations or corporate property, both real and personal, shall never be relinquished or suspended, and all corporations in this State or doing business therein, shall be subject to taxation for State, county, school, municipal, and other purposes, on real and personal property owned or used by them, and not by this Constitution exempted from taxation within the territorial limits of the authority levying the tax.

SEC. 9. The rate of taxation of real and personal property for State purposes shall never exceed ten (10) mills on each dollar of assessed valuation; and if the taxable property in the State shall amount to fifty million (50,000,000) dollars the rate shall not exceed five (5) mills on each dollar of valuation; and whenever the taxable property in the State shall amount to one hundred million (100,000,000) dollars, the rate shall not exceed three (3) mills on each dollar of valuation; and whenever the taxable property in the State shall amount to three hundred million (300,000,000) dollars the rate shall never thereafter exceed one and one-half (1½) mills on each dollar of valuation, unless a proposition to increase such rate, specifying the rate proposed and the time during which the same shall be levied, shall have been submitted to the people at a general election, and shall have received a majority of all the votes cast for and against it at such election.

SEC. 10. The making of profit, directly or indirectly, out of State, county, city, town, township, or school district money, or using the same for any purpose not authorized by law, by any public officer, shall be deemed a felony, and shall be punished as provided by law.

SEC. 11. No appropriation shall be made, nor any expenditure authorized by the Legislature, whereby the expenditure of the State during any fiscal year shall exceed the total tax then provided for by law, and applicable to such appropriation or expenditure unless the Legislature making such appropriation shall provide for levying a sufficient tax, not exceeding the rates allowed in section nine (9) of this article, to pay such appropriation or expenditure within such fiscal year. This provision shall not apply to appropriations or expenditures to suppress insurrection, defend the State, or assist in defending the United States in time of war.

SEC. 12. There shall be a State board of equalization, consisting of the Governor, Secretary of State, Attorney-General, State Auditor, and State Treasurer, whose duties shall be prescribed by law. The board of county commissioners for the several counties of the State, shall constitute boards of equalization for their respective counties, whose duty it shall be to equalize the valuation of the taxable property in the county, under such rules and regulations as shall be prescribed by law.

SEC. 13. No money shall be drawn from the treasury, but in pursuance of appropriations made by law.

SEC. 14. No money shall be drawn from the county treasuries except upon the warrant of a duly authorized officer, in such manner and form as shall be prescribed by the Legislature.

SEC. 15. The Legislature shall provide by law, such a system of county finance, as shall cause the business of the several counties to be conducted on a cash basis. It shall also provide that whenever any county shall have any warrants outstanding and unpaid, for the payment of which there are no funds in the county treasury, the county commissioners, in addition to other taxes provided by law, shall levy a special tax, not to exceed ten (10) mills on the dollar, of taxable property, as shown by the last preceding assessment, for the creation of a special fund for the redemption of said warrants; and after the levy of such special tax, all warrants issued before such levy shall be paid exclusively out of said fund. All moneys in the county treasury at the end of each fiscal year, not needed for current expenses, shall be transferred to said redemption fund.

Sec. 16. The Legislature shall pass all laws necessary to carry out the provisions of this article.

Article VIII

PUBLIC INDEBTEDNESS AND SUBSIDIES

Section 1. The Legislature shall not in any manner create any debt or debts, liability or liabilities, which shall singly or in the aggregate, exclusive of the debt of the Territory at the date of its admission as a State, exceed the sum of one and one-half per centum upon the assessed value of the taxable property in the State, except in case of war, to repel an invasion or suppress insurrection, unless the same shall be authorized by law for some single object or work to be distinctly specified therein, which law shall provide ways and means, exclusive of loans, for the payment of the interest of such debt or liability, as it falls due; and also for the payment and discharge of the principal of such debt or liability, within twenty years of the time of the contracting thereof, and shall be irrepealable until the principal and interest thereon shall be paid and discharged; but no such law shall take effect until at a general election it shall have been submitted to the people, and shall have received a majority of all the votes cast for and against it at such election; and all moneys raised by the authority of such law, shall be applied only to the specified object therein stated, or to the payment of the debt thereby created, and such law shall be published in at least one newspaper in each county, or city and county, if one be published therein, throughout the State, for three months next preceding the election at which it is submitted to the people. The Legislature may, at any time after the approval of such law, by the people, if no debt shall have been contracted in pursuance thereof, repeal the same.

Sec. 2. The credit of the State shall not, in any manner, be given, or loaned to, or in aid of any individual, association, municipality or corporation; nor shall the State directly or indirectly, become a stockholder in any association or corporation.

Sec. 3. No county, city, town, township, board of education, or school district, or other sub-division of the State, shall incur any indebtedness, or liability in any manner, or for any purpose, exceeding in that year, the income and revenue provided for it for such year, without the assent of two-thirds of the qualified electors thereof, voting at an election to be held for that purpose, nor unless, before or at the time of incurring such indebtedness provision shall be made for the collection of an annual tax sufficient to pay the interest on such indebtedness as it falls due, and also to constitute a sinking fund for the payment of the principal thereof, within twenty years from the time of contracting the same. Any indebtedness or liability incurred contrary to this provision shall be void: *Provided*, That this section shall not be construed to apply to the ordinary and necessary expenses authorized by the general laws of the State.

SEC. 4. No county, city, town, township, board of education, or school district, or other sub-division, shall lend, or pledge the credit or faith thereof directly or indirectly, in any manner, to, or in aid of any individual, association or corporation, for any amount or for any purpose whatever, or become responsible for any debt, contract or liability of any individual, association or corporation in or out of this State.

ARTICLE IX

EDUCATION AND SCHOOL LANDS

SECTION 1. The stability of a republican form of government depending mainly upon the intelligence of the people, it shall be the duty of the Legislature of Idaho, to establish and maintain a general, uniform and thorough system of public, free common schools.

SEC. 2. The general supervision of the public schools of the State shall be vested in a board of education, whose powers and duties shall be prescribed by law; the Superintendent of Public Instruction, the Secretary of State and Attorney-General, shall constitute the board, of which the Superintendent of Public Instruction shall be president.

SEC. 3. The public school fund of the State shall forever remain inviolate and intact; the interest thereon only shall be expended in the maintenance of the schools of the State, and shall be distributed among the several counties and school districts of the State in such manner as may be prescribed by law. No part of this fund, principal or interest, shall ever be transferred to any other fund, or used or appropriated except as herein provided. The State Treasurer shall be the custodian of this fund, and the same shall be securely and profitably invested as may be by law directed. The State shall supply all losses thereof that may in any manner occur.

SEC. 4. The public school fund of the State shall consist of the proceeds of such lands as have heretofore been granted, or may hereafter be granted, to the State by the general government, known as school lands, and those granted in lieu of such; lands acquired by gift or grant from any person or corporation, under any law or grant of the general government; and of all other grants of land or money made to the State from the general government for general educational purposes, or where no other special purpose is indicated in such grant; all estates or distributive shares of estates that may escheat to the State; all unclaimed shares and dividends of any corporation incorporated under the laws of the State; and all other grants, gifts, devises, or bequests made to the State for general educational purposes.

SEC. 5. Neither the Legislature, nor any county, city, town, township, school district, or other public corporation, shall ever make any appropriation, or pay from any public fund or moneys whatever, anything in aid of any church or sectarian, or religious society, or for any sectarian or religious purpose, or to help support or sustain any school, academy, seminary, college, university or other literary or scientific institution, controlled by any church or sectarian or religious denomination whatsoever; nor shall any grant or donation of land, money or other personal property ever be made by the State, or any such public corporation, to any church or for any sectarian or religious purpose.

SEC. 6. No religious test or qualification shall ever be required of any person as a condition of admission into any public educational institution of the State, either as teacher or student; and no teacher or student of any such institution shall ever be required to attend or participate in any religious service whatever. No sectarian or religious tenets or doctrines shall ever be taught in the public schools, nor shall any distinction or classification of pupils be made on account of race or color. No books, papers, tracts or documents of a political, sectarian or denominational character shall be used or introduced in any schools established under the provisions of this article, nor shall any teacher or any district receive any of the public school moneys in which the schools have not been taught in accordance with the provisions of this article.

SEC. 7. The Governor, Superintendent of Public Instruction, Secretary of State, and Attorney-General, shall constitute the State board of land commissioners, who shall have the direction, control and disposition of the public lands of the State, under such regulations as may be prescribed by law.

SEC. 8. It shall be the duty of the State board of land commissioners to provide for the location, protection, sale or rental of all the lands heretofore, or which may hereafter be, granted to the State by the general government, under such regulations as may be prescribed by law, and in such manner as will secure the maximum possible amount therefor: *Provided*, That no school lands shall be sold for less than ten (10) dollars per acre. No law shall ever be passed by the Legislature granting any privileges to persons who may have settled upon any such public lands, subsequent to the survey thereof by the general government, by which the amount to be derived by the sale, or other disposition of such lands, shall be diminished, directly or indirectly. The Legislature shall, at the earliest practicable period, provide by law that the general grants of land made by Congress to the State shall, be judiciously located and carefully preserved and held in trust, subject to disposal at public auction for the use and benefit of the respective objects for which said grants of land were made, and the Legislature shall provide for the sale of said lands from time to time, and for the sale of timber on all State lands, and for the faithful application of the proceeds thereof in accordance with the terms of said grants: *Provided*, That not to exceed twenty-five sections of school lands shall be sold in any one year, and to be sold in subdivisions of not to exceed one hundred and sixty (160) acres to any one individual, company or corporation.

SEC. 9. The Legislature may require by law that every child of sufficient mental and physical ability shall attend the public school throughout the period between the ages of six and eighteen years, for a time equivalent to three years, unless educated by other means.

SEC. 10. The location of the university of Idaho, as established by existing laws is hereby confirmed. All the rights, immunities, franchises, and endowments heretofore granted thereto by the Territory of Idaho are hereby perpetuated unto the said university. The Regents shall have the general supervision of the university, and the control and direction of all the funds of, and appropriations to, the university, under such regulations as may be prescribed by law. No university lands shall be sold for less than ten dollars per acre, and in subdivisions not to exceed one hundred and sixty acres, to any one person, company or corporation.

Sec. 11. The permanent educational funds, other than funds arising from the disposition of university lands belonging to the State, shall be loaned on first mortgage on improved farm lands within the State, or on State or United States bonds, under such regulations as the Legislature may provide: *Provided*, That no loan shall be made of any amount of money exceeding one-third of the market value of the lands at the time of the loan, exclusive of buildings.

Article X

PUBLIC INSTITUTIONS

Section 1. Educational, reformatory, and penal institutions, and those for the benefit of the insane, blind, deaf and dumb, and such other institutions as the public good may require, shall be established and supported by the State in such manner as may be prescribed by law.

Sec. 2. The seat of government of the State of Idaho shall be located at Boise City for twenty years from the admission of the State, after which time the Legislature may provide for its re-location, by submitting the question to a vote of the electors of the State at some general election.

Sec. 3. The Legislature may submit the question of the location of the seat of government to the qualified voters of the State at the general election, then next ensuing, and a majority of all the votes upon said question cast at said election shall be necessary to determine the location thereof. Said Legislature shall also provide that in case there shall be no choice of location at said election the question of choice between the two places for which the highest number of votes shall have been cast shall be submitted in like manner to the qualified electors of the State at the next general election.

Sec. 4. All property and institutions of the Territory, shall, upon adoption of the Constitution, become the property and institutions of the State of Idaho.

Sec. 5. The Governor, Secretary of State, and Attorney-General shall constitute a board, to be known as the State prison commissioners, and shall have the control, direction and management of the penitentiaries of the State. The Governor shall be chairman, and the board shall appoint a warden, who may be removed at pleasure. The warden shall have the power to appoint his subordinates, subject to the approval of the said board.

Sec. 6. There shall be appointed by the Governor three directors of the asylum for the insane, who shall be confirmed by the senate. They shall have the control, direction, and management of the said asylums, under such regulations as the Legislature shall provide, and hold their offices for a period of two years. The directors shall have the appointment of the medical superintendent, who shall appoint the assistants with the approval of the directors.

Sec. 7. The Legislature for sanitary reasons may cause the removal to more suitable localities of any of the institutions mentioned in section one of this article.

ARTICLE XI

CORPORATIONS, PUBLIC AND PRIVATE

SECTION 1. All existing charters or grants of special or exclusive privileges, under which the corporators or grantees shall not have organized or commenced business in good faith at the time of the adoption of this Constitution, shall thereafter have no validity.

SEC. 2. No charter of incorporation shall be granted, extended, changed or amended by special law, except for such municipal, charitable, educational, penal, or reformatory corporations as are or may be, under the control of the State; but the Legislature shall provide by general law for the organization of corporations hereafter to be created: *Provided*, That any such general law shall be subject to future repeal or alteration by the Legislature.

SEC. 3. The Legislature may provide by law for altering, revoking, or annulling any charter of incorporation existing and revocable at the time of the adoption of this Constitution, in such manner, however, that no injustice shall be done to the corporators.

SEC. 4. The Legislature shall provide by law that in all elections for directors or managers of incorporated companies, every stockholder shall have the right to vote in person or by proxy, for the number of shares of stock owned by him, for as many persons as there are directors or managers to be elected, or to cumulate said shares, and give one candidate as many votes as the number of directors multiplied by the number of his shares of stock, shall equal, or to distribute, them on the same principle among as many candidates as he shall think fit, and such directors shall not be elected in any other manner.

SEC. 5. All railroads shall be public highways, and all railroad, transportation, and express companies shall be common carriers, and subject to legislative control, and the Legislature shall have power to regulate and control by law, the rates of charges for the transportation of passengers and freight by such companies or other common carriers from one point to another in the State. Any association or corporation organized for, the purpose, shall have the right to construct and operate a railroad between any designated points within this State, and to connect within or at the State line with railroads of other States and Territories. Every railroad company shall have the right with its road, to intersect, connect with, or cross any other railroad, under such regulations as may be prescribed by law, and upon making due compensation.

SEC. 6. All individuals, associations, and corporations, similarly situated shall have equal rights to have persons or property transported on and over any railroad, transportation, or express route in this State, except that preference may be given to perishable property. No undue or unreasonable discrimination shall be made in charges or facilities for transportation of freight or passengers of the same class, by any railroad, or transportation, or express company, between persons or places within the State; but excursion or commutation tickets may be issued and sold at special rates, provided such rates are the same to all persons. No railroad, or transportation, or express company shall be allowed to charge, collect or receive, under penalties which the Legislature shall prescribe, any greater charge or toll for the transportation of freight or passengers, to any place or station upon its route or line, than it charges for the transportation of the same class of freight or passengers to any more distant place or station upon its route or line within this State. No railroad, express, or transportation company, nor any lessee, manager, or other employee thereof, shall give any preference to any individual, association, or corporation, in furnishing cars or motive power or for the transportation of money or other express matter.

SEC. 7. No corporation other than municipal corporations in existence at the time of the adoption of this Constitution, shall have the benefit of any future legislation, without first filing in the office of the Secretary of State an acceptance of the provisions of this Constitution in binding form.

SEC. 8. The right of eminent domain shall never be abridged, or so construed as to prevent the Legislature from taking the property and franchise of incorporated companies, and subjecting them to public use, the same as property of individuals; and the police powers of the State shall never be abridged or so construed as to permit corporations to conduct their business in such manner as to infringe the equal rights of individuals, or the general well-being of the State.

SEC. 9. No corporation shall issue stocks or bonds, except for labor done, services performed, or money or property actually received; and all fictitious increase of stock or indebtedness shall be void. The stock of corporations shall not be increased except in pursuance of general law, nor without the consent of the persons, holding a majority of the stock, first obtained at a meeting, held after at least thirty days' notice given in pursuance of law.

SEC. 10. No foreign corporation shall do any business in this State without having one or more known places of business, and, an authorized agent or agents in the same, upon whom process may be served, and no company or corporation formed under the laws of any other country, State, or Territory, shall have or be allowed to exercise or enjoy, within this State any greater rights or privileges than those possessed or enjoyed by corporations of the same or similar character created under the laws of this State.

SEC. 11. No street, or other railroad, shall be constructed within any city, town, or incorporated village without the consent of the local authorities having the control of the street or highway proposed to be occupied by such street or other railroad.

SEC. 12. The Legislature shall pass no law for the benefit of a railroad, or other corporation, or any individual or association of individuals retroactive in its operation, or which imposes on the people of any county or municipal subdivision of the State, a new liability in respect to transactions or considerations already past.

SEC. 13. Any association or corporation, or the lessees or managers thereof, organized for the purpose, or any individual, shall have the right to construct and maintain lines of telegraph or telephone within this State, and connect the same with other lines; and the Legislature shall by general law of uniform operation provide reasonable regulations to give full effect to this section.

Sec. 14. If any railroad, telegraph, express, or other corporation, organized under any of the laws of this State shall consolidate by sale or otherwise with any railroad, telegraph, express, or other corporation organized under any of the laws of any other State or Territory, or of the United States, the same shall not thereby become a foreign corporation, but the courts of this State shall retain jurisdiction over that part of the corporate property within the limits of the State in all matters that may arise, as if said consolidation had not taken place.

Sec. 15. The Legislature shall not pass any law permitting the leasing or alienation of any franchise so as to release or relieve the franchise or property held thereunder from any of the liabilities of the lessor or grantor, or lessee or grantee, contracted or incurred in the operation, use, or enjoyment of such franchise, or any of its privileges.

Sec. 16. The term " corporation " as used in this article, shall be held and construed to include all associations and joint stock companies having or exercising any of the powers or privileges of corporations not possessed by individuals or partnerships.

Sec. 17. Dues from private corporations shall be secured by such means as may be prescribed by law, but in no case shall any stockholder be individually liable in any amount over or above the amount of stock owned by him.

Sec. 18. That no incorporated company, or any association of persons or stock company, in the State of Idaho, shall directly or indirectly combine or make any contract with any other incorporated company, foreign or domestic, through their stockholders or the trustees or assignees of such stockholders, or in any manner whatsoever, for the purpose of fixing the price or regulating the production of any article of commerce or of produce of the soil, or of consumption by the people; and that the Legislature be required to pass laws for the enforcement thereof, by adequate penalties, to the extent, if necessary for that purpose, of the forfeiture of their property and franchise.

Article XII

CORPORATIONS—MUNICIPAL

Section 1. The Legislature shall provide by general laws for the incorporation, organization, and classification of the cities and towns, in proportion to the population, which laws may be altered, amended, or repealed by the general laws. Cities and towns heretofore incorporated, may become organized under such general laws, whenever a majority of the electors at a general election, shall so determine, under such provision therefor as may be made by the Legislature.

Sec. 2. Any county or incorporated city or town may make and enforce, within its limits, all such local, police, sanitary, and other regulations as are not in conflict with its charter or with the general laws.

Sec. 3. The State shall never assume the debts of any county, town, or other municipal corporation. unless such debts shall have been created to repel invasion, suppress insurrection or defend the State in war.

Sec. 4. No county, town, city, or other municipal corporation, by vote of its citizens or otherwise, shall ever become a stockholder in any joint stock company, corporation or association whatever, or raise money for, or make donation or loan its credit to, or in aid of, any such company or association: *Provided*, That cities and towns may contract indebtedness for school, water, sanitary, and illuminating purposes: *Provided*, That any city or town contracting such indebtedness shall own its just proportion of the property thus created, and receive from any income arising therefrom, its proportion to the whole amount so invested.

Article XIII

IMMIGRATION AND LABOR

Section 1. There shall be established a bureau of immigration, labor and statistics, which shall be under the charge of a commissioner of immigration, labor and statistics, who shall be appointed by the Governor, by and with the consent of the senate. The commissioner shall hold his office for two years, and until his successor shall have been appointed and qualified, unless sooner removed. The commissioner shall collect information upon the subject of labor, its relation to capital, the hours of labor and the earnings of laboring men and women, and the means of promoting their material, social, intellectual and moral prosperity. The commissioner shall annually make a report in writing to the Governor of the State of the information collected and collated by him, and containing such recommendations as he may deem calculated to promote the efficiency of the bureau.

Sec. 2. Not more than eight (8) hours' actual work shall constitute a lawful day's work on all State and municipal works.

Sec. 3. All labor of convicts confined in the State's prison shall be done within the prison grounds, except where the work is done on public works under the direct control of the State.

Sec. 4. The employment of children under the age of fourteen (14) years in underground mines is prohibited.

Sec. 5. No person, not a citizen of the United States, or who has not declared his intention to become such, shall be employed upon, or in connection with, any State or municipal works.

Sec. 6. The Legislature shall provide by proper legislation for giving to mechanics, laborers, and material men an adequate lien on the subject-matter of their labor.

Sec. 7. The Legislature may establish boards of arbitration, whose duty it shall be to hear and determine all differences and controversies between laborers and their employers which may be submitted to them in writing by all the parties. Such boards of arbitration shall possess all the powers and authority, in respect to administering oaths, subpœnaing witnesses, and compelling their attendance, preserving order during the sittings of the board, punishing for contempt, and requiring the production of papers and writings, and all other powers and privileges, in their nature applicable, conferred by law on justices of the peace.

Sec. 8. The commissioner of immigration, labor and statistics shall perform such duties and receive such compensation as may be prescribed by law.

Article XIV

MILITIA

SECTION 1. All able-bodied male persons, residents of this State, between the ages of eighteen and forty-five years, shall be enrolled in the militia, and perform such military duty as may be required by law; but no person having conscientious scruples against bearing arms, shall be compelled to perform such duty in time of peace. Every person claiming such exemption from service, shall, in lieu thereof, pay into the school fund of the county of which he may be a resident, an equivalent in money, the amount and manner of payment to be fixed by law.

SEC. 2. The Legislature shall provide by law for the enrollment, equipment and discipline of the militia, to conform as nearly as practicable to the regulations for the government of the armies of the United States, and pass such laws to promote volunteer organizations as may afford them effectual encouragement.

SEC. 3. All militia officers shall be commissioned by the Governor, the manner of their selection to be provided by law, and may hold their commissions for such period of time as the Legislature may provide.

SEC. 4. All military records, banners, and relics of the State, except when in lawful use, shall be preserved in the office of the adjutant-general as an enduring memorial of the patriotism and valor of the soldiers of Idaho; and it shall be the duty of the Legislature to provide by law for the safe-keeping of the same.

SEC. 5. All military organizations under the laws of this State shall carry no other device, banner, or flag than that of the United States or the State of Idaho.

SEC. 6. No armed police force, or detective agency, or armed body of men, shall ever be brought into this State for the suppression of domestic violence, except upon the application of the Legislature, or the executive when the Legislature cannot be convened.

Article XV

WATER RIGHTS

SECTION 1. The use of all waters now appropriated, or that may hereafter be appropriated for sale, rental, or distribution; also of all water originally appropriated for private use, but which after such appropriation has heretofore been, or may hereafter be sold, rented, or distributed, is hereby declared to be a public use, and subject to the regulation and control of the State in the manner prescribed by law.

SEC. 2. The right to collect rates or compensation for the use of water supplied to any county, city, or town, or water district, or the inhabitants thereof, is a franchise, and can not be exercised except by authority of and in the manner prescribed by law.

SEC. 3. The right to divert and appropriate the unappropriated waters of any natural stream to beneficial uses, shall never be denied. Priority of appropriation shall give the better right as between those using the water; but when the waters of any natural stream are not sufficient for the service of all those desiring the use of the same, those using the water for domestic purposes shall (subject to such limitations as may be prescribed by law) have the preference over those claiming for any other purpose; and those using the water for agricultural purposes shall have preference over those using the same for manufacturing purposes. And in any organized mining district, those using the water, for mining purposes, or milling purposes connected with mining, shall have preference over those using the same for manufacturing or agricultural purposes. But the usage by such subsequent appropriators shall be subject to such provisions of law regulating the taking of private property for public and private use, as referred to in section fourteen of Article I, of this Constitution.

SEC. 4. Whenever any waters have been, or shall be, appropriated or used for agricultural purposes, under a sale, rental, or distribution thereof, such sale, rental, or distribution shall be deemed an exclusive dedication to such use; and whenever such waters so dedicated shall have once been sold, rented, or distributed to any person who has settled upon or improved land for agricultural purposes with the view of receiving the benefit of such water under such dedication, such person, his heirs, executors, administrators, successors, or assigns, shall not thereafter, without his consent, be deprived of the annual use of the same, when needed for domestic purposes, or to irrigate the land so settled upon or improved, upon payment therefor, and compliance with such equitable terms and conditions as to the quantity used and times of use, as may be prescribed by law.

SEC. 5. Whenever more than one person has settled upon, or improved land with the view of receiving water for agricultural purposes, under a sale, rental or distribution thereof, as in the last preceding section of this article, provided, as among such persons priority in time shall give superiority of right to the use of such water in the numerical order of such settlements or improvements; but whenever the supply of such water shall not be sufficient to meet the demands of all those desiring to use the same, such priority of right shall be subject to such reasonable limitations as to the quantity of water used and times of use as the Legislature, having due regard, both to such priority of right and the necessities of those subsequent in time of settlement or improvement, may by law prescribe.

SEC. 6. The Legislature shall provide by law the manner in which reasonable maximum rates may be established to be charged for the use of water sold, rented or distributed for any useful or beneficial purpose.

ARTICLE XVI

LIVE-STOCK

SECTION 1. The Legislature shall pass all necessary laws to provide for the protection of livestock against the introduction or spread of pleuro-pneumonia, glanders, splenetic or Texas fever, and other infectious or contagious diseases. The Legislature may also establish a system of quarantine or inspection, and such other regulations as may be necessary for the protection of stock-owners and most conducive to the stock interests within this State.

ARTICLE XVII

STATE BOUNDARIES

SECTION 1. The name of this State is Idaho, and its boundaries are as follows: Beginning at a point in the middle channel of the Snake river where the northern boundary of Oregon intersects the same; then follow down the channel of Snake river to a point opposite the mouth of the Kooskooskia or Clearwater river; thence due north to the forty-ninth parallel of latitude; thence east along that parallel to the thirty-ninth degree of longitude west of Washington; thence south along that degree of longitude to the crest of the Bitter Root Mountains; thence southward along the crest of the Bitter Root Mountains till its intersection with the Rocky Mountains; thence southward along the crest of the Rocky Mountains to the thirty-fourth degree of longitude west of Washington; thence south along that degree of longitude to the forty-second degree of north latitude; thence west along that parallel to the eastern boundary of the State of Oregon; thence north along that boundary to the place of beginning.

ARTICLE XVIII

COUNTY ORGANIZATION

SECTION 1. The several counties of the Territory of Idaho as they now exist, are hereby recognized as legal subdivisions of this State.

SEC. 2. No county seat shall be removed unless upon petition of a majority of the qualified electors of the county, and unless two-thirds of the qualified electors of the county, voting on the proposition at a general election, shall vote in favor of such removal. A proposition of removal of the county seat shall not be submitted in the same county more than once in six years, except as provided by existing laws. No person shall vote at any county seat election who has not resided in the county six months, and in the precinct ninety days.

SEC. 3. No county shall be divided unless a majority of the qualified electors of the territory proposed to be cut off, voting on the proposition at a general election, shall vote in favor of such division: *Provided*, That this section shall not apply to the creation of new counties. No person shall vote at such election who has not been ninety days a resident of the territory proposed to be annexed. When any part of a county is stricken off and attached to another county, the part stricken off shall be held to pay its ratable proportion of all then existing liabilities of the county from which it is taken.

SEC. 4. No new county shall be established which shall reduce any county to an area of less than four hundred square miles, nor shall a new county be formed containing an area of less than four hundred square miles.

SEC. 5. The Legislature shall establish, subject to the provisions of this article, a system of county governments which shall be uniform throughout the State; and by general laws shall provide for township or precinct organization.

SEC. 6. The Legislature, by general and uniform laws, shall provide for the election biennially in each of the several counties of the State, of county commissioners, a sheriff, county treasurer, who is ex-officio public administrator; probate judge, who is ex-officio county superintendent of public instruction; county assessor, who is ex-officio tax collector; a coroner and a surveyor. The clerk of the district court shall be ex-officio auditor and recorder. No other county offices shall be established, but the Legislature by general and uniform laws shall provide for the election of such township, precinct and municipal officers as public convenience may require, and shall prescribe their duties and fix their terms of office. The Legislature shall provide for the strict accountability of county, township, precinct and municipal officers for all fees which may be collected by them, and for all public and municipal moneys which may be paid to them, or officially come into their possession. The county commissioners may employ counsel when necessary. The sheriff, auditor and recorder and clerk of the district court shall be empowered by the county commissioners to appoint such deputies and clerical assistance as the business of their offices may require; said deputies and clerical assistance to receive such compensation as may be fixed by the county commissioners. No sheriff or county assessor shall be qualified to hold the term of office immediately succeeding the term for which he was elected.

Sec. 7. The officers provided by section six (6) of this article shall receive annually as compensation for their services as follows: Sheriff, not more than four thousand dollars and not less than one thousand dollars, together with such mileage as may be prescribed by law; clerk of the district court, who is ex-officio auditor and recorder, not more than three thousand dollars and not less than five hundred dollars; probate judge, who is ex-officio county superintendent of public instruction, not more than two thousand dollars and not less than five hundred dollars; county assessor, who is ex-officio tax collector, not more than three thousand dollars and not less than five hundred dollars; county treasurer, who is ex-officio public administrator, not more than one thousand dollars, and not less than three hundred dollars; coroner, not more than five hundred dollars; county surveyor, not more than one thousand dollars; county commissioners, such per diem and mileage as may be prescribed by law; and justices of the peace and constables such fees as may be prescribed by law.

Sec. 8. The compensation provided in section seven (7) for the officers therein mentioned shall be paid by fees or commissions, or both, as prescribed by law. All fees and commissions received by such officers in excess of the maximum compensation per annum provided for each in section seven (7) of this article shall be paid to the county treasurer for the use and benefit of the county. In case the fees received in any one year by any one such officers shall not amount to the minimum compensation per annum therein provided, he shall be paid by the county a sum sufficient to make his aggregate annual compensation equal to such minimum compensation.

Sec. 9. The neglect or refusal of any officer named in this article to account for and pay into the county treasury any money received as fees or compensation in excess of the maximum amount allowed to such officer by the provisions of this article, within forty days after the receipt of the same, shall be a felony, and the grade of the crime shall be the embezzlement of public moneys, and be punishable as provided for such offense.

SEC. 10. The board of county commissioners shall consist of three members, whose term of office shall be two years.

SEC. 11. County, township and precinct officers shall perform such duties as shall be prescribed by law.

ARTICLE XIX

APPORTIONMENT

SECTION 1. Until otherwise provided by law the apportionment of the two houses of the Legislature shall be as follows:

The first senatorial districts shall consist of the county of Shoshone, and shall elect two senators.

The second shall consist of the counties of Kootenai and Latah, and shall elect one senator.

The third shall consist of the counties of Nez Perce and Idaho, and shall elect one senator.

The fourth shall consist of the counties of Nez Perce and Latah, and shall elect one senator.

The fifth shall consist of the county of Latah, and shall elect one senator.

The sixth shall consist of the county of Boise, and shall elect one senator.

The seventh shall consist of the county of Custer, and shall elect one senator.

The eighth shall consist of the county of Lemhi, and shall elect one senator.

The ninth shall consist of the county of Logan, and shall elect one senator.

The tenth shall consist of the county of Bingham, and shall elect one senator.

The eleventh shall consist of the counties of Bear Lake, Oneida and Bingham, and shall elect one senator.

The twelfth shall consist of the counties of Owyhee and Cassia, and shall elect one senator.

The thirteenth shall consist of the county of Elmore, and shall elect one senator.

The fourteenth shall consist of the county of Alturas, and shall elect one senator.

The fifteenth shall consist of the county of Ada, and shall elect two senators.

The sixteenth shall consist of the county of Washington, and shall elect one senator.

SEC. 2. The several counties shall elect the following members of the house of representatives:

The county of Ada, three members.

The counties of Ada and Elmore, one member.

The county of Alturas, two members.

The county of Boise, two members.

The county of Bear Lake, one member.

The county of Bingham, three members.

The county of Cassia, one member.

The county of Custer, two members.

The county of Elmore, one member.
The county of Idaho, one member.
The counties of Idaho and Nez Perce, one member.
The county of Kootenai, one member.
The county of Latah, two members.
The counties of Kootenai and Latah, one member.
The county of Logan, two members.
The county of Lemhi, two members.
The county of Nez Perce, one member.
The county of Oneida, one member.
The county of Owyhee, one member.
The county of Shoshone, four members.
The county of Washington, two members.
The counties of Bingham, Logan and Alturas, one member.

Article XX

AMENDMENTS

Section 1. Any amendment or amendments to this Constitution may be proposed in either branch of the Legislature, and if the same shall be agreed to by two-thirds of all the members of each of the two houses, voting separately, such proposed amendment or amendments shall, with the yeas and nays thereon, be entered on their journals, and it shall be the duty of the Legislature to submit such amendment or amendments to the electors of the State at the next general election, and cause the same to be published without delay for at least six consecutive weeks, prior to said election, in not less than one newspaper of general circulation published in each county; and if a majority of the electors shall ratify the same, such amendment or amendments shall become a part of this Constitution.

Sec. 2. If two or more amendments are proposed, they shall be submitted in such manner that the electors shall vote for or against each of them separately.

Sec. 3. Whenever two-thirds of the members elected to each branch of the Legislature shall deem it necessary to call a convention to revise or amend this Constitution, they shall recommend to the electors to vote at the next general election for or against a convention, and if a majority of all the electors voting at said election shall have voted for a convention, the Legislature shall at the next session provide by law for calling the same; and such convention shall consist of a number of members not less than double the number of the most numerous branch of the Legislature.

Sec. 4. Any Constitution adopted by such convention, shall have no validity until it has been submitted to, and adopted by the people.

Article XXI

SCHEDULE AND ORDINANCE

Section 1. That no inconvenience may arise from a change of the Territorial government to a permanent State government, it is declared that all writs, actions, prosecutions, claims, liabilities, and obligations against the Territory of Idaho, of whatsoever nature, and rights of individuals, and of bodies corporate, shall continue as if no change had taken place in this government; and all process which may, before the organization of the judicial department under this Constitution, be issued under the authority of the Territory of Idaho, shall be as valid as if issued in the name of the State.

SEC. 2. All laws now in force in the Territory of Idaho which are not repugnant to this Constitution shall remain in force until they expire by their own limitation or be altered or repealed by the Legislature.

SEC. 3. All fines, penalties, forfeitures, and escheats accruing to the Territory of Idaho shall accrue to the use of the State.

SEC. 4. All recognizances, bonds, obligations, or other undertakings heretofore taken, or which may be taken before the organization of the judicial department under this Constitution, shall remain valid, and shall pass over to and may be prosecuted in the name of the State; and all bonds, obligations, or other undertaking executed by this Territory, or to any other officer in his official capacity, shall pass over to the proper State authority, and to their successors in office, for the uses therein respectively expressed, and may be sued for and recovered accordingly. All criminal prosecutions and penal actions which have arisen, or which may arise before the organization of the judicial department under this Constitution, and which shall then be pending, may be prosecuted to judgment and execution in the name of the State.

SEC. 5. All officers, civil and military, now holding their offices and appointments in this Territory under the authority of the United States, or under the authority of this Territory, shall continue to hold and exercise their respective offices and appointments until suspended under this Constitution.

SEC. 6. This Constitution shall be submitted for adoption or rejection, to a vote of the electors qualified by the laws of this Territory to vote at all elections at an election to be held on the Tuesday next after the first Monday in November, A. D. 1889. Said election shall be conducted in all respects in the same manner as provided by the laws of the Territory for general election, and the returns thereof shall be made and canvassed in the same manner and by the same authority as provided in cases of such general elections, and abstracts of such returns duly certified shall be transmitted to the board of canvassers now provided by law for canvassing the returns of votes for Delegate in Congress. The said canvassing board shall canvass the votes so returned and certify and declare the result of said election in the same manner, as is required by law for the election of said Delegate.

At the said election the ballots shall be in the following form: For the Constitution—yes; no.

And as a heading to each of said ballots shall be printed on each ballot, the following instructions to voters:

All persons who desire to vote for the Constitution, or any of the articles submitted to a separate vote, may erase the word " no."

All persons who desire to vote against the Constitution, or against any article submitted separately, may erase the word " yes."

Any person may have printed or written on his ballot only the words, " For the Constitution " or "Against the Constitution," and such ballots shall be counted for or against the Constitution accordingly.

Sec. 7. This Constitution shall take effect and be in full force immediately upon the admission of the Territory as a State.

Sec. 8. Immediately upon the admission of the Territory as a State, the Governor of the Territory, or in case of his absence or failure to act, the secretary of the Territory, or in case of his absence or failure to act, the president of this convention, shall issue a proclamation, which shall be published, and a copy thereof mailed to the chairman of the board of county commissioners of each county, calling an election by the people of all State, district, county, township, and other officers, created and made elective by this Constitution, and fixing a day for such election, which shall not be less than forty days after the date of such proclamation, nor more than ninety days after the admission of the Territory as a State.

Sec. 9. The board of commissioners of the several counties shall thereupon order such election for said day, and shall cause notice thereof to be given, in the manner and for the length of time provided by the laws of the Territory in cases of general elections for Delegate to Congress and county and other officers. Every qualified elector of the Territory, at the date of said election, shall be entitled to vote thereat. Said election shall be conducted in all respects in the same manner as provided by the laws of the Territory for general elections, and returns thereof shall be made and canvassed in the same manner and by the same authority as provided in cases of such general election; but returns for all State and district officers and members of the Legislature, shall be made to the canvassing board hereinafter provided for.

Sec. 10. The Governor, Secretary, Controller, and Attorney-General of the Territory, and the president of this convention, or a majority of them, shall constitute a board of canvassers to canvass the vote at such elections for all State and district officers and members of the Legislature. The said board shall assemble at the seat of government of the Territory, on the thirtieth day after the date of such election (or on the following day if such day fall on Sunday), and proceed to canvass the votes for all State and district officers and members of the Legislature, in the manner provided by the laws of the Territory for canvassing the vote for Delegate to Congress, and they shall issue certificates of election to the persons found to be elected to said offices severally, and shall make and file with the Secretary of the Territory an abstract certified by them, of the number of votes cast for each person for each of said offices, and of the total number of votes cast in each county.

Sec. 11. The canvassing boards of the several counties shall issue certificates of election to the several persons found by them to have been elected to the several county and precinct offices.

Sec. 12. All officers elected at such election shall, within thirty days after they have been declared elected, take the oath required by this Constitution, and give the same bond required by the law of the Territory to be given in case of like officers of the Territory, district or county, and shall thereupon enter upon the duties of their respective offices; but the Legislature may require by law all such officers to give other or further bonds as a condition of their continuance in office.

SEC. 13. All officers elected at said election, shall hold their offices until the Legislature shall provide by law, in accordance with this Constitution, for the election of their successors, and until such successors shall be elected and qualified.

SEC. 14. The Governor-elect of the State, immediately upon his qualifying and entering upon the duties of his office, shall issue his proclamation convening the Legislature of the State at the seat of government on a day to be named in said proclamation and which shall not be less than thirty nor more than sixty days after the date of such proclamation. Within ten days after the organization of the Legislature both houses of the Legislature shall then and there proceed to elect, as provided by law, two Senators of the United States for the State of Idaho. At said election, the two persons who shall receive the majority of all the votes cast by said senators and representatives, shall be elected as such United States Senators, and shall be so declared by the presiding officers of said joint session. The presiding officers of the senate and house, shall issue a certificate to each of said senators, certifying his election, which certificates shall also be signed by the Governor and attested by the Secretary of State.

SEC. 15. The Legislature shall pass all necessary laws to carry into effect the provisions of this Constitution.

SEC. 16.. Whenever any two of the judges of the supreme court of the State, elected under the provisions of this Constitution, shall have qualified in their offices, the causes then pending in the supreme court of the Territory, and the papers, records, and proceedings of said court, and the seal and other property pertaining thereto, shall pass into the jurisdiction and possession of the supreme court of the State; and until so superceded the supreme court of the Territory and the judges thereof shall continue, with like powers and jurisdiction, as if this Constitution had not been adopted. Whenever the judge of the district court of any district, elected under the provisions of this Constitution, shall have qualified in office, the several causes then pending in the district court of the Territory, within any county in such district, and the records, papers, and proceedings of said district court, and the seal and other property pretaining thereto, shall pass into the jurisdiction and possession of the district court of the State for such county; and until the district courts of this Territory shall be superceded in the manner aforesaid the said district courts and the judges thereof shall continue with the same jurisdiction and power to be exercised in the same judicial districts respectively, as heretofore constituted under the laws of the Territory.

SEC. 17. Until otherwise provided by law, the seals now in use in the supreme and district courts of this Territory are hereby declared to be the seals of the supreme and district courts, respectively, of the State.

SEC. 18. Whenever this Constitution shall go into effect, the books, records, and papers, and proceedings of the probate court in each county, and all causes and matters of administration and other matters pending therein, shall pass into the jurisdiction and possession of the probate court of the same county of the State, and the said probate court shall proceed to final decree or judgment, order, or other determination in the said several matters and causes as the said probate court might have done as if this Constitution had not been adopted.

SEC. 19. It is ordained by the State of Idaho that perfect toleration of religious sentiment shall be secured, and no inhabitant of said State shall ever be molested in person or property on account of his or her mode of religious worship. And the people of the State of Idaho do agree and declare that we forever disclaim all right and title to the unappropriated public lands lying within the boundaries thereof, and to all lands lying within said limits, owned or held by any Indians or Indian tribes; and until the title thereto shall have been extinguished by the United States, the same shall be subject to the disposition of the United States, and said Indian lands shall remain under the absolute jurisdiction and control of the Congress of the United States; that the lands belonging to citizens of the United States, residing without the said State of Idaho, shall never be taxed at a higher rate than the lands belonging to the residents thereof. That no taxes shall be imposed by the State on the lands or property therein belonging to, or which may hereafter be purchased by, the United States, or reserved for its use. And the debts and liabilities of this Territory shall be assumed and paid by the State of Idaho. That this ordinance shall be irrevocable, without the consent of the United States and the people of the State of Idaho.

SEC. 20. That in behalf of the people of Idaho, we, in convention assembled, do adopt the Constitution of the United States.

Done in open convention, at Boise City, in the Territory of Idaho, this sixth day of August, in the year of our Lord one thousand eight hundred and eighty-nine.

WM. H. CLAGETT, *President.*

SELECTED DOCUMENTS

The documents selected for this section have been chosen to illustrate the various attitudes, concerns and issues in the development of Idaho. Documents relating specifically to the constitutional development of Idaho will be found in volume three of <u>Sources and Documents of United States Constitutions</u>, a companion reference collection to the Columbia University volumes previously cited.

TERRITORIAL PERIOD

The Idaho Territory developed slowly but steadily in the decade after the Civil War, and particularly after the Indian wars were largely settled. The original gold rush had led to a mining economy extending to other mineral resources which were systematically sought out and developed, while in the southern areas along the Snake River irrigated farming was introduced. The growth of the southern region, however, was punctuated with religious conflicts as both Mormon and anti-Mormon elements moved north from Utah, or the Mormon state of Deseret, into Idaho. Violent hostility toward the increasing numbers of Chinese laborers led to a massacre of Chinese in the town of Pierce in 1885. Political antipathy toward Mormons resulted in a territorial test oath the same year, aimed at preventing Mormons from voting or serving on juries.

Act of March 3, 1863

Territory of Idaho established.
Boundaries.

Be it enacted by the Senate and House of Representatives of the United States of America in Congress assembled, That all that part of the territory of the United States included within the following limits, to wit: Beginning at a point in the middle channel of the Snake River where the northern boundary of Oregon intersects the same ; then follow down said channel of Snake River to a point opposite the mouth of the Kooskooskia, or Clear Water River ; thence due north to the forty-ninth parallel of latitude ; thence east along said parallel to the twenty-seventh degree of longitude west of Washington ; thence south along said degree of longitude to the northern boundary of Colorado Territory ; thence west along said

boundary to the thirty-third degree of longitude west of Washington;
thence north along said degree to the forty-second parallel of latitude;
thence west along said parallel to the eastern boundary of the State of
Oregon; thence north along said boundary to place of beginning. And
the same is hereby created into a temporary government, by the name of
the Territory of Idaho: *Provided*, That nothing in this act contained shall
be construed to inhibit the Government of the United States from dividing
said Territory or changing its boundaries in such manner and at such
time as Congress shall deem convenient and proper, or from attaching
any portion of said Territory to any other state or territory of the United
States: *Provided, further*, That nothing in this act contained shall be
construed to impair the rights of person or property now pertaining to the
Indians in said Territory, so long as such rights shall remain unextin-
guished by treaty between the United States and such Indians, or to
include any territory which, by treaty with any Indian tribes, is not, without the consent of said tribe, to be included within the territorial limits or
jurisdiction of any state or territory; but all such territory shall be excepted out of the boundaries, and constitute no part of the Territory of
Idaho, until said tribe shall signify their assent to the President of the
United States to be included within said Territory, or to affect the authority of the Government of the United States to make any regulations
respecting such Indians, their lands, property, or other rights, by treaty,
law, or otherwise, which it would have been competent for the Government to make if this act had never passed.

Boundaries may be changed.

Indian rights not impaired.

SEC. 2. *And be it further enacted*, That the executive power and authority in and over said Territory of Idaho shall be vested in a governor,
who shall hold his office for four years, and until his successor shall be
appointed and qualified, unless sooner removed by the President of the
United States. The governor shall reside within said Territory, and shall
be commander-in-chief of the militia, and superintendent of Indian affairs
thereof. He may grant pardons and respites for offences against the laws
of said Territory, and reprieve for offences against the laws of the United
States until the decision of the President of the United States can be
made known thereon; he shall commission all officers who shall be appointed to office under the laws of the said Territory, and shall take care
that the laws be faithfully executed.

Executive power of terri-tory.
Governor.

SEC. 3. *And be it further enacted*, That there shall be a secretary of
said Territory, who shall reside therein, and shall hold his office for four
years, unless sooner removed by the President of the United States; he
shall record and preserve all laws and proceedings of the legislative
assembly hereinafter constituted, and all the acts and proceedings of the
governor in his executive department; he shall transmit one copy of the
laws and journals of the legislative assembly within thirty days after the
end of each session, and one copy of the executive proceedings and official
correspondence semiannually, on the first days of January and July in
each year, to the President of the United States, and two copies of the
laws to the President of the Senate and to the Speaker of the House of
Representatives for the use of Congress; and in case of the death, removal, resignation, or absence of the governor from the Territory, the
secretary shall be, and he is hereby, authorized and required to execute
and perform all the powers and duties of the governor during such vacancy or absence, or until another governor shall be duly appointed and
qualified to fill such vacancy.

Secretary.

When to act as governor.

SEC. 4. *And be it further enacted*, That the legislative power and
authority of said Territory shall be vested in the governor and a legislative assembly. The legislative assembly shall consist of a council and
house of representatives. The council shall consist of seven members
having the qualifications of voters as hereinafter prescribed, whose term
of service shall continue two years. The house of representatives shall,

Legislative power.
Assembly.
Council.

House of representatives. at its first session, consist of thirteen members possessing the same qualifications as prescribed for the members of the council, and whose term of service shall continue one year. The number of representatives may be increased by the legislative assembly, from time to time, to twenty six, in proportion to the increase of qualified voters; and the council, in

Apportionment. like manner, to thirteen. An apportionment shall be made as nearly equal as practicable among the several counties or districts for the election of the council and representatives, giving to each section of the Territory representation in the ratio of its qualified voters as nearly as may be. And the members of the council and of the house of representatives shall reside in, and be inhabitants of, the district or county, or counties, for

Census. which they may be elected respectively. Previous to the first election, the governor shall cause a census or enumeration of the inhabitants and qualified voters of the several counties and districts of the Territory to be taken by such persons and in such mode as the governor shall designate and appoint, and the persons so appointed shall receive a reasonable

First election. compensation therefor. And the first election shall be held at such time and places, and be conducted in such manner both as to the persons who shall superintend such election and the returns thereof, as the governor shall appoint and direct; and he shall, at the same time, declare the number of members of the council and house of representatives to which each of the counties or districts shall be entitled under this act. The

Plurality of votes to elect. persons having the highest number of legal votes in each of said council districts for members of the council shall be declared by the governor to be duly elected to the council; and the persons having the highest number of legal votes for the house of representatives shall be declared by the governor to be duly elected members of said house: *Provided,* That in case two or more persons voted for shall have an equal number of votes, and in case a vacancy shall otherwise occur in either branch of the legislative assembly, the governor shall order a new election; and the persons thus elected to the legislative assembly shall meet at such place and on

Subsequent elections. such day as the governor shall appoint; but thereafter the time, place, and manner of holding and conducting all elections by the people, and the apportioning the representation in the several counties or districts to the council and house of representatives, according to the number of qualified voters, shall be prescribed by law, as well as the day of the commencement of the regular sessions of the legislative assembly: *Provided,*

Length of sessions of assembly. That no session in any one year shall exceed the term of forty days, except the first session, which may continue sixty days.

Voters at first election, SEC. 5. *And be it further enacted,* That every free white male inhabitant above the age of twenty-one years, who shall have been an actual resident of said Territory at the time of the passage of this act, shall be entitled to vote at the first election, and shall be eligible to any office

at subsequent elections. within the said Territory; but the qualifications of voters, and of holding office, at all subsequent elections, shall be such as shall be prescribed by the legislative assembly.

Legislative power. SEC. 6. *And be it further enacted,* That the legislative power of the Territory shall extend to all rightful subjects of legislation consistent with the Constitution of the United States and the provisions of this act; but no law shall be passed interfering with the primary disposal of the soil;

Taxes. no tax shall be imposed upon the property of the United States, nor shall the lands or other property of non-residents be taxed higher than the lands or other property of residents. Every bill which shall have passed the council and house of representatives of the said Territory shall, be-

Veto power of governor. fore it becomes a law, be presented to the governor of the Territory; if he approve, he shall sign it: but if not, he shall return it, with his objections, to the house in which it originated, who shall enter the objections at large upon their journal and proceed to reconsider it. If, after such reconsideration, two thirds of that house shall agree to pass the bill, it shall be sent, together with the objections, to the other house, by which it shall likewise be reconsidered; and if approved by two thirds of that house, it shall become a law. But in all such cases the votes of both houses shall be determined by yeas and nays, to be entered on the journal of each house respectively. If any bill shall not be returned by the governor within three days (Sunday excepted) after it shall have been presented to him, the same shall be a law in like manner as if he had signed it, unless the assembly, by adjournment, prevent its return; in which case it shall not be a law : *Provided*, That whereas slavery is prohibited in said territory by act of Congress of June nineteenth, eighteen hundred and sixty-two, nothing herein contained shall be construed to authorize or permit its existence therein.

Veto power.

Slavery.
1862, ch. 111.
Ante, p. 432.

SEC. 7. *And be it further enacted,* That all township, district, and county officers, not herein otherwise provided for, shall be appointed or elected, as the case may be, in such manner as shall be provided by the governor and legislative assembly of the Territory of Idaho. The governor shall nominate and, by and with the advice and consent of the legislative council, appoint all officers not herein otherwise provided for; and in the first instance the governor alone may appoint all said officers, who shall hold their offices until the end of the first session of the legislative assembly, and shall lay off the necessary districts for members of the council and house of representatives, and all other officers.

Township, district, and county officers.

:-SEC. 8. *And be it further enacted,* That no member of the legislative assembly shall hold or be appointed to any office which shall have been created, or the salary or emoluments of which shall have been increased, while he was a member, during the term for which he was elected, and for one year after the expiration of such term ; but this restriction shall not be applicable to members of the first legislative assembly ; and no person holding a commission or appointment under the United States, except postmasters, shall be a member of the legislative assembly, or shall hold any office under the government of said Territory.

Members of legislative assembly not to hold, &c., certain offices.

Who may not be member of the assembly, or hold office.

SEC. 9. *And be it further enacted,* That the judicial power of said territory shall be vested in a supreme court, district courts, probate courts, and in justices of the peace. The supreme court shall consist of a chief justice and two associate justices, any two of whom shall constitute a quorum, and who shall hold a term at the seat of government of said Territory annually; and they shall hold their offices during the period of four years, and until their successors shall be appointed and qualified. The said Territory shall be divided into three judicial districts, and a district court shall be held in each of said districts by one of the justices of the supreme court at such times and places as may be prescribed by law; and the said judges shall, after their appointments, respectively, reside in the districts which shall be assigned them. The jurisdiction of the several courts herein provided for, both appellate and original, and that of the probate courts and of justices of the peace, shall be limited by law: *Provided,* That justices of the peace shall not have jurisdiction of any matter in controversy when the title or boundaries of land may be in dispute, or where the debt or sum claimed shall exceed one hundred dollars; and the said supreme and district courts, respectively, shall possess chancery as well as common-law jurisdiction. Each district court, or the judge thereof, shall appoint its clerk, who shall also be the register in chancery, and shall keep his office at the place where the court may be held. Writs of error, bills of exceptions, and appeals, shall be allowed in all cases from the final decisions of said district courts to the supreme court, under such regulations as may be prescribed by law. The supreme court, or the justices thereof, shall appoint its own clerk, and every clerk shall hold his office at the pleasure of the court for which he shall have been appointed. Writs of error and appeals from the final decisions of said supreme court shall be allowed, and may be taken to the supreme court

Judicial power.

Supreme court.

District courts and districts.

Justices of the peace.

Chancery powers.

Clerks of court.

Writs of error, &c.

Clerks.

Writs of error, &c.

Writs of error, appeals. of the United States, in the same manner and under the same regulations as from the circuit courts of the United States, where the value of the property or the amount in controversy, to be ascertained by the oath or affirmation of either party, or other competent witnesses, shall exceed one thousand dollars, except that a writ of error or appeal shall be allowed to the supreme court of the United States from the decision of the said supreme court created by this act, or of any judge thereof, or of the district courts created by this act, or of any judge thereof, upon any write of habeas corpus involving the question of personal freedom. And each of **Jurisdiction of district courts.** the said district courts shall have and exercise the same jurisdiction, in all cases arising under the Constitution and laws of the United States, as is vested in the circuit and district courts of the United States; and the **Precedence of trials.** first six days of every term of said courts, or so much thereof as shall be necessary, shall be appropriated to the trial of causes arising under the said Constitution and laws; and writs of error and appeal in all such cases shall be made to the supreme court of said Territory, the same as in **Fees of clerks.** other cases. The said clerks shall receive, in all such cases, the same fees which the clerks of the district courts of Washington Territory now receive for similar services.

Attorney. SEC. 10. *And be it further enacted,* That there shall be appointed an attorney for said territory, who shall continue in office four years, and until his successor shall be appointed and qualified, unless sooner removed by the President of the United States, and who shall receive the same fees and salary as the attorney of the United States for the present Territory of Washington. There shall also be a marshal for the Territory ap- **Marshal.** pointed, who shall hold his office for four years, and until his successor shall be appointed and qualified, unless sooner removed by the President of the United States, and who shall execute all processes issuing from the said courts when exercising their jurisdiction as circuit and district courts of the United States; he shall perform the duties, be subject to the same regulations and penalties, and be entitled to the same fees as the marshal of the district court of the United States for the present Territory of Washington, and shall, in addition, be paid two hundred dollars annually as a compensation for extra services.

Appointment of territorial officers. SEC. 11. *And be it further enacted,* That the governor, secretary, chief justice, and associate justices, attorney, and marshal, shall be appointed by the President of the United States, by and with the advice and consent of the Senate. The governor and secretary to be appointed as **Oath of office.** aforesaid, shall, before they act as such, respectively, take an oath or affirmation before the district judge or some justice of the peace in the limits of said Territory duly authorized to administer oaths and affirmations by the laws now in force therein, or before the chief justice or some associate justice of the supreme court of the United States, to support the Constitution of the United States, and faithfully to discharge the duties of their respective offices, which said oaths, when so taken, shall be certified by the person by whom the same shall have been taken; and such certificates shall be received and recorded by the said secretary among the executive proceedings; and the chief justice and associate justices, and all civil officers in said Territory, before they act as such, shall take a like oath or affirmation before the said governor or secretary, or some judge or justice of the peace of the Territory, who may be duly commissioned and qualified, which said oath or affirmation shall be certified and transmitted by the person taking the same to the secretary, to be by him recorded as aforesaid; and afterwards the like oath or affirmation shall be taken, certified, and recorded in such manner and form as may be pre- **Salaries.** scribed by law. The governor shall receive an annual salary of two thousand five hundred dollars, the chief justice and associate justices shall receive an annual salary of two thousand five hundred dollars, the secretary shall receive an annual salary of two thousand dollars; the said

---

salaries shall be paid quarter-yearly, from the dates of the respective appointments, at the treasury of the United States; but no payment shall be made until said officers shall have entered upon the duties of their respective appointments. The members of the legislative assembly shall be entitled to receive four dollars each per day, during their attendance at the sessions thereof, and four dollars each for every twenty miles' travel in going to and returning from said sessions, estimated according to the nearest usually travelled route, and an additional allowance of four dollars per day shall be paid to the presiding officer of each house for each day he shall so preside. And a chief clerk, one assistant clerk, one engrossing and one enrolling clerk, a sergeant-at-arms and doorkeeper may be chosen for each house; and the chief clerk shall receive four dollars per day, and the said other officers three dollars per day, during the session of the legislative assembly; but no other officers shall be paid by the United States: *Provided,* That there shall be but one session of the legislative assembly annually, unless, on an extraordinary occasion, the governor shall think proper to call the legislative assembly together. There shall be appropriated annually the usual sum to be expended by the governor to defray the contingent expenses of the Territory, including the salary of the clerk of the executive department; and there shall also be appropriated annually a sufficient sum, to be expended by the secretary of the Territory, and upon an estimate to be made by the Secretary of the Treasury of the United States, to defray the expenses of the legislative assembly, the printing of the laws, and other incidental expenses; and the governor and secretary of the Territory shall, in the disbursement of all moneys intrusted to them, be governed solely by the instructions of the Secretary of the Treasury of the United States, and shall, semi-annually, account to the said Secretary for the manner in which the aforesaid moneys shall have been expended; and no expenditure shall be made by said legislative assembly for objects not specially authorized by the acts of Congress making the appropriations, nor beyond the sums thus appropriated for such objects.

SEC. 12. *And be it further enacted,* That the legislative assembly of the Territory of Idaho shall hold its first session at such time and place in said Territory as the governor thereof shall appoint and direct; and at said first session, or as soon thereafter as they shall deem expedient, the governor and legislative assembly shall proceed to locate and establish the seat of government for said Territory at such place as they may deem eligible: *Provided,* That the seat of government fixed by the governor and legislative assembly shall not be at any time changed, except by an act of the said assembly duly passed, and which shall be approved, after due notice, at the first general election thereafter, by a majority of the legal votes cast on that question.

SEC. 13. *And be it further enacted,* That a delegate to the House of Representatives of the United States, to serve for the term of two years, who shall be a citizen of the United States, may be elected by the voters qualified to elect members of the legislative assembly, who shall be entitled to the same rights and privileges as are exercised and enjoyed by the delegates from the several other territories of the United States to the said House of Representatives; but the delegate first elected shall hold his seat only during the term of the Congress to which he shall be elected. The first election shall be held at such time and places, and be conducted in such manner as the governor shall appoint and direct; and at all subsequent elections the times, places, and manner of holding the elections shall be prescribed by law. The person having the greatest number of legal votes shall be declared by the governor to be duly elected, and a certificate thereof shall be given accordingly. That the Constitution and all laws of the United States which are not locally inapplicable shall have the same force and effect within the said Territory of Idaho as elsewhere within the United States.

Public lands in the Territory.

SEC. 14. *And be it further enacted,* That when the lands in the said Territory shall be surveyed, under the direction of the government of the United States, preparatory to bringing the same into market, sections

School sections reserved.

numbered sixteen and thirty-six in each township in said territory shall be, and the same are hereby, reserved for the purpose of being applied to schools in said Territory, and in the states and territories hereafter to be erected out of the same.

Judicial districts and assignments of judges.

SEC. 15. *And be it further enacted,* That, until otherwise provided by law, the governor of said Territory may define the *define the* judicial districts of said Territory, and assign the judges who may be appointed for said Territory to the several districts, and also appoint the times and places for holding courts in the several counties or subdivisions in each of said judicial districts, by proclamation to be issued by him; but the legislative assembly, at their first or any subsequent session, may organize. alter, or modify such judicial districts, and assign the judges, and alter the times and places of holding the courts, as to them shall seem proper and convenient.

Officers to give security for moneys intrusted to them for disbursement.

SEC. 16. *And be it further enacted,* That all officers to be appointed by the President of the United States, by and with the advice and consent of the Senate, for the Territory of Idaho, who, by virtue of the provisions of any law now existing, or which may be enacted by Congress, are required to give security for moneys that may be intrusted with them for disbursement, shall give such security at such time and in such manner as the Secretary of the Treasury may prescribe.

Treaties, &c., with Indian tribes, to be faithfully observed.

SEC. 17. *And be it further enacted,* That all treaties, laws, and other engagements made by the Government of the United States with the Indian tribes inhabiting the Territory embraced within the provisions of this act, shall be faithfully and rigidly observed, anything contained in this

Agencies and superintendencies continued.

act to the contrary notwithstanding; and that the existing agencies and superintendencies of said Indians be continued with the same powers and duties which are now prescribed by law, except that the President of the

Location may be changed.

United States may, at his discretion, change the location of the office of said agencies or superintendents.

APPROVED, March 3, 1863.

———

Act of Admission of July 3. 1890

Whereas, The people of the Territory of Idaho did, on the fourth day of July, eighteen hundred and eighty-nine, by a convention of delegates called and assembled for that purpose, form for themselves a constitution, which constitution was ratified and adopted by the people of said Territory at an election held therefor on the first Tuesday in November, eighteen hundred and eighty-nine, which constitution is republican in form and is in conformity with the Constitution of the United States; and *Preamble.*

Whereas, Said convention and the people of said Territory have asked the admission of said Territory into the Union of States on an equal footing with the original States in all respects whatever: Therefore,

Be it enacted by the Senate and House of Representatives of the United States of America in Congress assembled, That the State of Idaho is hereby declared to be a State of the United States of America, and is hereby declared admitted into the Union on an equal footing with the original States in all respects whatever; and that the constitution which the people of Idaho have formed for themselves be, and the same is hereby, accepted, ratified, and confirmed. *Idaho admitted as a new State.*

Constitution ratified, etc.

SEC. 2. That the said State shall consist of all the Territory described as follows: Beginning at the intersection of the thirty-ninth meridian with the boundary line between the United States and the British Possessions, then following said meridian south until it reaches the summit of the Bitter Root Mountains; thence southeastward along the crest of the Bitter Root range and the continental divide until it intersects the meridian of thirty-four degrees of longitude; thence southward on this meridian to the forty second parallel of latitude; thence west on this parallel of latitude to its intersection with a meridian drawn through the mouth of the Owyhee River; north on this meridian to the mouth of the Owyhee River; thence down the mid-channel of the Snake River to the mouth of the Clearwater River; and thence north on the meridian which passes through the mouth of the Clearwater to the boundary-line between the United States and the British Possessions, and east on said boundary-line to the place of beginning. *State boundaries.*

SEC. 3. That until the next general census, or until otherwise provided by law, said State shall be entitled to one Representative in the House of Representatives of the United States and the election of the Representative to the Fifty-first Congress and the Representative to the Fifty-second Congress shall take place at the time and be conducted and certified in the same manner as is provided in the constitution of the State for the election of State, district, and other officers in the first instance. The law of the Territory of Idaho for the registration of voters shall apply to the first election of State, District, and other officers held after the admission of the State of Idaho. County and precinct officers elected at the first election held after the admission of the State Idaho, shall assume the duties of their respective offices on the second Monday of January eighteen hundred and ninety-one. *Congressional representation.*

Election of Representative to Fifty-first and Fifty-second Congresses.

First State, etc., election.

County and precinct officers.

SEC. 4. That sections numbered sixteen and thirty-six in every township of said State, and where such sections, or any parts thereof, have been sold or otherwise disposed of by or under the authority of any act of Congress, other lands equivalent thereto, in legal subdivisions of not less than one quarter section, and as contiguous as may be to the section in lieu of which the same is taken, are hereby granted to said State for the support of common schools, such indemnity lands to be selected within said State in such manner as the legislature may provide, with the approval of the Secretary of the Interior. *School lands granted.*

Sale of school lands.   SEC. 5. That all lands herein granted for educational purposes shall be disposed of only at public sale, the proceeds to constitute a permanent school fund, the interest of which only shall be expended in the support of said schools. But said lands may, under such

Leases, etc.   regulations as the legislature shall prescribe, be leased for periods of not more than five years, and such lands shall not be subject to pre-emption, homestead entry, or any other entry under the land laws of the United States, whether surveyed or unsurveyed, but shall be reserved for school purposes only.

Lands for public buildings.   SEC. 6. That fifty sections of the unappropriated public lands within said State, to be selected and located in legal subdivisions as provided in section four of this act, shall be, and are hereby, granted to said State for the purpose of erecting public buildings at the capital of said State for legislative, executive, and judicial purposes.

Five per cent. of net proceeds, sales of public lands, for common schools fund.   SEC. 7. That five per centum of the proceeds of the sales of public lands lying within said State which shall be sold by the United States subsequent to the admission of said State into the Union, after deducting all the expenses incident to the same, shall be paid to the said State, to be used as a permanent fund, the interest of which only shall be expended for the support of the common schools within said State.

University lands to vest in State, etc. Vol. 21, p. 326.   SEC. 8. That the lands granted to the Territory of Idaho by the act of February eighteenth, eighteen hundred and eighty-one, entitled "An act to grant lands to Dakota, Montana, Arizona, Idaho, and Wyoming for university purposes," are hereby vested in the State of Idaho to the extent of the full quantity of seventy-two sections to said State, and any portion of said lands that may not have been selected by said Territory of Idaho may be selected by the said State;

Vol. 21, p. 326, amended. Minimum price of university lands. Proceeds to constitute a university fund.   but said act of February eighteenth, eighteen hundred and eighty-one, shall be so amended as to provide that none of said lands shall be sold for less than ten dollars per acre, and the proceeds shall constitute a permanent fund to be safely invested and held by said State, and the income thereof be used exclusively for university purposes.

State control of schools, etc. Sectarian, etc., schools, etc., not to be supported from proceeds of sales of school lands, etc.   The schools, colleges, and universities provided for in this act shall forever remain under the exclusive control of the said State, and no part of the proceeds arising from the sale or disposal of any lands herein granted for educational purposes shall be used for the support of any sectarian or denominational school, college, or university.

Penitentiary at Boise City, etc., granted to State.   SEC. 9. That the penitentiary at Boise City, Idaho, and all lands connected therewith and set apart and reserved therefor, and unexpended appropriations of money therefor, and the personal property of the United States now being in the Territory of Idaho, which has been in use in the said Territory in the administration of the Territorial government, including books and records and the property used at the constitutional convention which convened at Boise City, in the month of July, eighteen hundred and eighty-nine, are hereby granted and donated to the State of Idaho.

Lands for agricultural colleges. Ante, p. 215.   SEC. 10. That ninety thousand acres of land, to be selected and located as provided in section four of this act, are hereby granted to said State for the use and support of an agricultural college in said

Vol. 12, pp. 503-505.   State, as provided in the acts of Congress making donations of lands for such purposes.

Lands for internal improvements, etc.   SEC. 11. That in lieu of the grant of land for purposes of internal improvement made to the new States by the eighth section of the

Vol. 5, p. 455, repealed as to Idaho.   act of September fourth, eighteen hundred and forty-one, which section is hereby repealed as to the State of Idaho, and in lieu of any

Certain bounty and swamp, etc., lands. Vol. 9, pp. 520, 521. R. S., sec. 2479, p. 453, not extended to Idaho.   claim or demand by the said State under the act of September twenty-eighth eighteen hundred and fifty, and section twenty four hundred and seventy nine of the Revised Statutes, making a grant of swamp and overflowed lands to certain States, which grant it is hereby declared is not extended to the State of Idaho, and in lieu of any

Saline lands.   grant of saline lands to said State the following grants of lands are hereby made, to wit: To the State of Idaho: For the establishment and maintenance of a scientific school. one hundred thousand acres: For State normal schools, one hundred thousand acres; for the support and maintenance of the insane-asylum located at Blackfoot, fifty thousand acres; for the support and maintenance of the State University located at Moscow, fifty thousand acres; for the support and maintenance of the penitentiary located at Boise City, fifty thousand acres; for other State, charitable, educational, penal, and reformatory institutions, one hundred and fifty thousand acres. None of the lands granted by this act shall be sold for less than ten dollars an acre. *Specific lieu-land grants. Scientific school. Normal schools. Insane asylum. State University. Penitentiary Other State institutions. Minimum price of lands.*

SEC. 12. That the State of Idaho shall not be entitled to any further or other grants of land for any purpose than as expressly provided in this act. And the lands granted by this section shall be held, appropriated, and disposed of exclusively for the purpose herein mentioned, in such manner as the legislature of the State may provide. *No further grants. Limited to specified uses.*

SEC. 13. That all mineral lands shall be exempted from the grants by this act. But if sections sixteen and thirty-six, or any subdivision, or portion of any smallest subdivision thereof in any township shall be found by the Department of the Interior to be mineral lands, the said State is hereby authorized and empowered to select, in legal subdivisions, an equal quantity of other unappropriated lands in said State, in lieu thereof, for the use and the benefit of the common schools of said State. *Mineral lands exempt. Lands in lieu.*

SEC. 14. That all lands granted in quantity or as indemnity by this act shall be selected, under the direction of the Secretary of the Interior. from the surveyed unreserved, and unappropriated public lands of the United States within the limits of the State entitled thereto. And there shall be deducted from the number of acres of land donated by this act for specific objects to said State the number of acres heretofore donated by Congress to said Territory for similar objects. *Selections to be under direction of Secretary of the Interior. Deductions.*

SEC. 15. That the sum of twenty eight thousand dollars, or so much thereof as may be necessary, is hereby appropriated, out of any money in the Treasury not otherwise appropriated, for defraying the expenses of said convention and for the payment of the members thereof, under the same rules and regulations and at the same rates as are now provided by law for the payment of the Territorial legislatures, and for elections held therefor and thereunder. Any money hereby appropriated not necessary for such purpose shall be covered into the Treasury of the United States. *Appropriation for convention expenses, etc.*

SEC. 16. That the said State shall constitute a judicial district, the name thereof to be the same as the name of the State; and the circuit and district courts therefor shall be held at the capital of the State for the time being, and the said district shall, for judicial purposes, until otherwise provided. be attached to the ninth judicial circuit. There shall be appointed for said district one district judge, one United States attorney, and one United States marshal. The judge of the said district shall receive a yearly salary of three thousand five hundred dollars, payable in four equal installments, on the first days of January, April. July, and October of each year, and shall reside in the district. There shall be appointed clerks of said courts, in the said district, who shall keep their offices at the capital of said State. The regular terms of said courts shall be held in said district, at the place aforesaid. on the first Monday in April and the first Monday in November of each year, and only one grand jury and one petit jury shall be summoned in both said circuit and district courts. The circuit and district courts for said district, and the judges thereof, respectively, shall possess the same powers and jurisdiction, and perform the same duties required to be performed by the other circuit and district courts and judges of the United States, and shall be governed by the same laws and regulations. *Circuit and district courts established. Judge, attorney, marshal. Clerks. Terms. Juries. Jurisdiction, etc.*

Powers, etc., of officers. The marshal, district attorney, and clerks of the circuit and district courts of said district, and all other officers and persons performing duties in the administration of justice therein, shall severally possess the powers and perform the duties lawfully possessed and required to be performed by similar officers in other districts of the United States; and shall, for the services they may perform, receive **Fees, etc.** the fees and compensation allowed by law to other similar officers and persons performing similar duties in the State of Oregon.

Cases pending in the Supreme Court. SEC. 17. That all cases of appeal or writ of error heretofore prosecuted and now pending in the Supreme Court of the United States upon any record from the supreme court of said Territory, or that may hereafter lawfully be prosecuted upon any record from said court, may be heard and determined by said Supreme Court of the **Final proceedings.** United States; and the mandate of execution or of further proceedings shall be directed by the Supreme Court of the United States to the circuit or district court hereby established within the said State from or to the supreme court of such State, as the nature of **Territorial supreme court to be succeeded by circuit, district, and State courts.** the case may require. And the circuit, district, and State courts herein named shall, respectively, be the successors of the supreme court of the Territory, as to all such cases arising within the limits embraced within the jurisdiction of such courts, respectively, with full power to proceed with the same, and award mesne or final process **Judgments prior to admission.** therein; and that from all judgments and decrees of the supreme court of the Territory mentioned in this act, in any case arising within the limits of the proposed State prior to admission, the parties to such judgment shall have the same right to prosecute appeals and writs of error to the Supreme Court of the United States as they shall have had by law prior to the admission of said State into the Union.

Transfer of pending actions, etc. SEC. 18. That in respect to all cases, proceedings, and matters now pending in the supreme or district courts of the said Territory at the time of the admission into the Union of the State of Idaho and **Circuit and district courts.** arising within the limits of such State, whereof the circuit or district courts by this act established might have had jurisdiction under the laws of the United States had such courts existed at the time of the commencement of such cases, the said circuit and district courts, respectively, shall be the successors of said supreme and district **State courts.** courts of said Territory; and in respect to all other cases, proceedings, and matters pending in the supreme or district courts of said Territory at the time of the admission of such Territory into the Union, arising within the limits of said State, the courts established by such State shall, respectively, be the successors of said supreme **Transfer of files, records, etc.** and district Territorial courts; and all the files, records, indictments, and proceedings relating to any such cases shall be transferred to such circuit, district, and State courts, respectively, and the same **Writs, etc., not to abate, etc.** shall be proceeded with therein in due course of law; but no writ, action, indictment, cause, or proceeding now pending, or that prior to the admission of the State shall be pending, in any Territorial court in said Territory, shall abate by the admission of such State into the Union, but the same shall be transferred and proceeded within the proper United States circuit, district, or State court as **Proviso.** the case may be: *Provided, however,* That in all civil actions, causes, and proceedings in which the United States is not a party transfers **Request for trial in Federal courts, etc.** shall not be made to the circuit and district courts of the United States, except upon written request of one of the parties to such action or proceeding filed in the proper court; and in the absence of such request such cases shall be proceeded with in the proper State courts.

Operation of United States laws. SEC. 19. That from and after the admission of said State into the Union, in pursuance of this act, the laws of the United States not locally inapplicable shall have the same force and effect within the said State as elsewhere within the United States.

Sec. 20. That the legislature of the said State may elect two Senators of the United States as is provided by the constitution of said State, and the Senators and Representative of said State shall be entitled to seats in Congress and to all the rights and privileges of Senators and Representatives of other States in the Congress of the United States.

Election of United States Senators, etc.

Sec. 21. That until the State officers are elected and qualified under the provisions of the constitution of said State, the officers of the Territory of Idaho shall discharge the duties of their respective offices under the constitution of the State, in the manner and form as therein provided; and all laws in force made by said Territory, at the time of its admission into the Union, shall be in force in said State, except as modified or changed by this act or by the constitution of the State.

Territorial officers to hold over, etc., until after State election.

Existing Territorial laws.

Sec. 22. That all acts or parts of acts in conflict with the provisions of this act, whether passed by legislature of said Territory or by Congress, are hereby repealed.

Repeal provision.

Approved, July 3, 1890.

UNIFICATION OF THE STATE'S EDUCATIONAL SYSTEM

The historical development of educational systems in various states is discussed in detail, followed by a description of the utilization of the higher education resources in Idaho.

Source: New England Magazine, May, 1911

THE UNIFICATION OF A STATE'S EDUCATIONAL FORCES

By GEORGE EDWIN MacLEAN, Ph.D., LL.D.,

President of the State University of Iowa

IN the 20th century economy, efficiency, and ethics call for the unification of a State's educational forces. The age of competition has been succeeded by that of co-operation and even of combination. The economist's dictum that "planless production makes waste" educators, sometimes under the stimulus of legislators, are learning to apply. Within the last two years not less than five states have passed noteworthy legislation in the direction of unifying their educational systems. In the United States the State and not the Nation, or the local district, town, or county, happily is the educational unit. The progress of educational unification becomes the more significant when we name the five states —Florida, West Virginia, Massachusetts, New York and Iowa.

In Florida the Governor has appointed a commission, consisting of the Presidents of the State institutions, the President of one private college, three school superintendents, three high school principals, to act with the State Superintendent of Public Instruction in formulating measures advocated in an educational campaign for the following purposes: 1. The teaching of Agriculture and Home Economics in the high schools of the State. 2. A compulsory school law. 3. The constitutional amendment for the millage tax, one-half for the support of the State University and State College for Women, and one-half to supplement the income of the county high schools. 4. Modifications of the course of study so as to articulate with the College of the University.

In West Virginia a State Board of Regents, which has not been in office for one year, has the educational control of all the educational institutions of the State, including the University. The President of this Board is the State Superintendent of Instruction. The University has recently appointed a professor of secondary education, whose chief duty is to give encouragement and help in the organization of high schools throughout the state, and who also acts as inspector of high schools, representing in this capacity the State Department of Schools. The University, normal schools, preparatory schools, and high schools of the State are thus being better articulated, and brought into closer and more sympathetic co-operation.

Massachusetts, in some sense the mother of and leader in American education, establishing the first State University in 1636, (now known as Harvard), and a decade later requiring every town of 100 families to maintain a school that would prepare for the University, and with a school system reformed by Horace Mann last year effected nothing less than a legislative educational revolution. It was in the interest of educational unification, and precipitated by the vital mistake in 1906 of establishing a Commission on Industrial Education distinct from the State Board of Education. The separation of the proposed trade schools from the public schools threatened schism in the public school system. The resulting agitation overthrow the organization of years in the interest of educational unification by the establishment of a Board of Education of nine persons appointed by the Governor with the advice and consent of the council in classes of three for terms of three years. The members of the Board serve without compensation. The Industrial Commission was abolished. The old-time Secretaryship of the Board of Education was changed into a Commissioner of Education appointed by the Board for a term of five years. He was made the executive officer of the Board with plenary powers and supervision of all educational work supported in whole or in part by the Commonwealth. He was aided by two deputy commissioners, one of whom was qualified to deal with industrial education. The Pilgrim tendency in Massachusetts to extreme individualism, and the emphasis upon the town as a unit mark a contrast in Massachusetts leadership in education with that of New York.

The progress, therefore, of unification in Massachusetts is perhaps more noteworthy than the marvelous advances which culminated this year in New York State. New York had the earliest framework for state educational unity. In 1784 in their Assembly, "the first session after peace," leaders like George Clinton, the Livingstones, John Jay, and Alexander Hamilton, presented a plan providing for the University of the State of New York. Dr. Draper well says: "It was the first movement in America to organize the educational work of a State upon a nonpolitical, nonsectarian, and every way nonexclusive basis which would bring the sovereign authority and the financial aid of the state to the practical support of education that should be unlimited and free. It is not too much to say that it was the first really strong educational conception in America, and that it was by a group of men than which there has not been a greater in the land.

"The plan at first provided that the Board of Regents should be legally possessed of all the properties and should exercise the powers of appointment and all the other governing powers over all colleges and schools. But it was immediately seen that this would not work, and a reform was initiated in the Board itself. This reform provided for separate and local boards of trustees in all the institutions, with all the powers over

property, courses, appointments, and administration. The "University" was to be a supervisory university. * * * * The idea was to bind all together, and bind all to the state, to the end that the newer and weaker institutions might have the fraternal aid of the older and stronger ones, and that all the people and every part of the state might have the uplifting influence of this general organization of the more advanced institutions of learning in the state. In other words, New York was setting up a state organization supervisory of her higher learning."

As early as 1787 plans were under way to enlarge the supervision of the Board of Regents to include academies as well as colleges, and to provide state aid. The plan has worked well with reference to the secondary schools, but it had soon to be modified with reference to the colleges, owing to disputes as to the prerogative of the Board of Regents and the Board of Trustees of Columbia, and later of other colleges. In the words of Dr. Draper "The purpose of the founders of the state to make Columbia a state college and the mother of many colleges and schools which should together constitute a real state university" was defeated. "It was doubtless inevitable, and probably necessary, but surely it was a heavy penalty both upon the state and the college, for the inability of a few men to adjust their official powers so as to make a workable and effective educational organization. * * * There were losses all around but they were doubtless necessary for college individuality and freedom had to be." Nevertheless the unifying influences of the Board of Regents of the University of New York, largely a mere examining board, were such as to cause the Board of Regents to be imbedded in the new Constitution of the State in 1894.

The Educational Unification Act of 1904 abolished the office of State Superintendent of Public Instruction, and established that of Commissioner of Education, making it possible for the Board of Regents with the Commissioner to have control over the elementary school system. ••••

•••• In 1857 the Constitution of the State then adopted, provided for a State Board of Education, embracing all the educational interests of the state, including common schools. This board consisted of the Governor, Lieutenant-Governor, and one member from each judicial district.

In the same year Horace Mann and the Chancellor of the University as an educational commission reported "that they could not regard any system of public instruction as complete without some liberal provision for institutions of higher learning." They provided "free scholarships, subject to obligation to teach in the State University." They proposed "to open the doors of the University to a large class who desired to fit themselves for the common pursuits of life." They wished by "their plan of organization to make use of the University for elevating conditions of the primary schools of the state * * * and to stimulate the youth to attain the proud distinction of being prepared for the State University." They "desired to send into every family of Iowa a spirit-stirring impulse and to arouse the latent energies of every young spirit and thus carry forward the common school system to the completest realization of its glorious mission."

A partial fulfillment of this dream of a "glorious mission" came in the establishment, first, of a certificate, and then of an accrediting system for high schools and academies, by which their graduates could be admitted to the University without examination. Inspection of the schools brought a living touch and inspiration in the visit of the professor or inspector to the high schools. The articulation of the high schools with the University, as regards courses of study, was effected by an early statute in Iowa, by which the University was "to begin subjects where the high schools left off." This is giving an unexpected, and perhaps, a happy result. Flexibility of admission requirements is thus forced upon the University, as well as an impetus to do everything within its power to help the schools to maintain standards. This should tend to dissipate the common

notion that the University dictates to the High School, grounded upon the great influence of the college in New England in dominating the secondary school. In the case of the Western State University it might well be queried, if one falls into the spirit of complaint, whether the high school has not dictated more to the University than the University to the high school. In fact, where these institutions are an integral part of a great state system with a migration of pupils and teachers from one to the other, there tends to be a reciprocal and personal relation. Indeed the time is now at hand when a prophecy made by President Judson in 1893 at the Williams College Centennial is being fulfilled: "Every course of study in every secondary school shall always lead directly to some course of study in some college." This does not mean that every college is to be filled with multitudinous courses, but it does make for a state University as the co-ordinating point in that it should have some college or course to complete all courses, cultural, commercial, or industrial, of the secondary schools.

It is interesting to note that the Iowa State Board of Education, doubtless created primarily to correlate the State University and the separate College of Agriculture, and State Teachers College, has among its earliest acts found it necessary to create a board known as the Board on Secondary School Relations, composed of the Inspector of the secondary schools as chairman, and three other members, one chosen from the faculty of the College of Liberal Arts of the State University, one from the faculty of the State College of Agriculture and Mechanic Arts, and one from the faculty of the State Teachers College. The faculty representatives on this Board are appointed by the Presidents of the respective institutions and approved by the State Board of Education. Private and denominational colleges desiring to co-operate are encouraged to do so. The loose practice of admitting graduates of non-accredited high schools on probation is done away with, students from such schools being required to take the entrance examination on entering, and thus

84

IDAHO

the value of the accredited relation is further heightened. The fact that the Iowa State Board of Education finds practically an organic relation between these three institutions and the secondary schools, and takes action though the statute creating the Board has not the remotest reference to secondary schools, is a demonstration of the progress of educational unification.

In another direction there exists an intimate inter-relation of educational forces in bodies like the Board of Agriculture, of Geology, of Educational Examiners, of the Library Commission. Wisely, in North Dakota the Geological Survey is under the Board of Trustees of the University, as is also the Public Health Laboratory, the Biological Station at Devils Lake, and the Mining sub-station at Hebron. These things are indicative of a great comprehensive plan of co-operation, and a fuller recognition of the unity actually existing will give a state-wide educational system. Indeed, in Iowa after the passage of the act establishing a State Board of Education, a bill was introduced extending their powers so as to include the government of the Geological Survey, the State Library, the Traveling Library, the Iowa Historical department, the State Historical Society, and the Hall of Public Archives. This was a manifestation of the consciousness that all educational activities of the State should be correlated. It may be a sign of an on-coming of a fourth branch of government co-ordinated with the three established—executive, legislative and judicial; namely, the educational.

The educational forces of a state are much wider than state institutions. The church and private schools and colleges, the learned and philanthropic societies, the organizations of business, of labor, and of women, call for co-operation and a possible federation. The private schools and colleges recognizing credits from state institutions, and having their credits received by state institutions, and oftentimes by various co-operative devices and exchanges of professors, illustrate that there is a Republic of Letters within the body politic. Without technical legal relations there is an underlying educa-

tional organism. It is clear there is no occasion for antagonism among state-supported, church, or private bodies, and yet there is often waste of energy from lack of understanding, from unnecessary duplication, and inconvenience to migrating students.

All are watching with interest the unification of educational forces as exemplified by the association of Wesley College of North Dakota with the State University. It would seem a splendid example to set for the newer states that are not embarrassed, like the older states, by the interests that center about long-established institutions. One is constrained by the logic of the statement of President Robertson: "In the last analysis, those who found the state university and those who found church colleges are one and the same people. There is no organic union. The unity of ideal of their common founders assures co-operation of agencies to secure unity in the joint product. * * The separation of church and state is preserved in the full authority to teach and in the administration of funds. Only wasteful competition is eliminated. The 'Church' and 'state' are made to appear what they really are—not separate, antagonistic organisms, but simply two specialized forms of activity of one and the same people." We hope to catch the spirit of your association in the older states, and as in Great Britain colleges widely separated in space are federated into one University, we hope to have a greater University than that by law established, consisting of all colleges and schools in the state in co-operation.

It is plainly possible by voluntary co-operation and federation for institutions to unify the educational forces of the state. Indeed associations like the North Central Association of Colleges and Secondary Schools, for a great group of states, have been able to bring about a practical comity, co-operation, and establishment of standards. How much more might this be possible within a limited territory like a state! The popular assemblies, like the State Teachers' Association, with their departments and educational councils, open the way for closer relations that might be stronger even than legal ones. The Iowa experiment has begun with a *governmental* relation, and limited to the three higher institutions. Already the governmental and lay board is wisely recognizing the need of an expert council in the establishment of the Board on Secondary School Relations, which sprang out of the recommendations of a Committee of Fifteen from the three faculties, five from each institution. Herein is the suggestion of an academic council. While the twenty states, which, like Iowa, separated their College of Agriculture from the State University, watch and wisely *wait* the working out of the experiment of governmental unification in Iowa, might not these states vigorously try other experiments less radical. Suppose the governing bodies of the separate institutions and the faculties founded a conference for certain common purposes? In such a case the public, private and church institutions might seek a confederacy. The public institutions might persuade a legislature to have a standing and visiting committee. Certainly those who object to governmental co-ordination, which springs out of the attempt for educational unification, might attempt some voluntary efficient way. They rightly press the need of preserving the individuality of the different kinds of institutions, and the enthusiasm of their special patrons. They fear tendencies to compel dead uniformity, to seek an average, or the maiming of this or that institution in the desire to avoid unnecessary duplication. Let them be equally zealous in positive measures for co-ordination. Is it too much to hope that the vision of an ideal Republic of Letters within the State, an *imperium in imperio*, will, if not in this generation, ultimately be fulfilled? Why should not these states in the Middle West lead the way?

The elements are at hand for a combination of the unified system of the State of New York with the best in the system of a western state having a great State University, filling the gap in the New York state system. A commissioner of education, not a political officer like the State Superintendent, would be a

minister of education, or educational statesman, worthy to be what the Chancellor of the University of Nebraska is called in the statutes "the chief educator." As the Commissioner of Education in New York is *ex officio* a member of the Board of Trustees of Cornell, in part a State University, so should this commissioner be a member of the governing boards of the state institutions of higher learning. Or possibly, better yet, with the proper evolution of the Presidency of the State University, when that officer is relieved by Deans of colleges who are virtually presidents of them, he might become the co-ordinating officer sought.

In conclusion, whatever may be the results of the interesting Iowa experiment in beginning the correlation with a representative common board of some size, on an honor basis, with its action focused by a Finance Committee, one thing is clear, that economy, efficiency, and sound education, and all the interests of the state from center to circumference demand the co-ordination of all public institutions. It is evident the happiest provision will include the co-operation with full state recognition of private institutions, and with the State University as the co-ordinating center, an institution at the furthest remove from all political, partisan and sectarian influences.

North Dakota has a splendid start to realize this ideal. Your University is like your new town named "Energy," pitched where there are immense deposits of lignite. The town promises to be an industrial center for mills of all kinds and electrical power plants. With the lignite coal electricity can be developed in enormous quantities and transmitted at low cost over a great area of your State. It is possible that the transmitted electric power will be running the gang plows and threshing outfits, stimulating the growth of crops, and lighting the farmers' houses, barns, dairy and even poultry houses.

The University, richly endowed and supported by the State to have the best experts and equipment in every department of knowledge, is the educational center. It is the state's central light and power plant with sub-stations in great sister institutions, public and private.

COUNTRY SCHOOLS FOR COUNTRY CHILDREN

This is a fine discussion of the country schools
as developed in Page County, Idaho. In addition a description of a boys' farm camp is presented with the
educational value of the program.

Source; World's Work, May, 1912.

COUNTRY SCHOOLS FOR COUNTRY CHILDREN

THE SIMPLE MOTTO BY WHICH MISS JESSIE FIELD HAS MADE A WONDERFUL TRANSFORMATION IN EDUCATION IN PAGE COUNTY, IOWA

BY

W. K. TATE

(STATE RURAL SCHOOL SUPERVISOR FOR SOUTH CAROLINA)

IT WAS my privilege recently to spend two days with Miss Jessie Field, County Superintendent of Education in Page County, Iowa, in an endeavor to discover the secret of the reputation that her schools have attained among the country schools of the United States. I found it in Miss Field herself, and in the application of her motto. "We must teach a country child in terms of country life."

Page County lies off the beaten travel routes, on the Missouri line in southwestern Iowa, and Clarinda, the county seat, is somewhat hard to reach. As our train moved leisurely through the fertile, rolling valley I saw everywhere the signs of rural prosperity. The homes and farm buildings were comfortable and attractive, the roads were fair, and the rural telephone was universal. The shocks of corn, the harrowed fields ready for the wheat crop, the hay stacks, the barrels of apples under

the trees that were being stripped of their red and golden burden, and the bluegrass pastures with their droves of cattle, hogs, and sheep, told a story of intelligent, diversified farming.

Miss Field herself greeted me at Clarinda; she was expecting my visit.

"Your train is late," she said, "but I have a runabout here, and we will have time to see one school before closing time."

Without further ceremony we stepped into a little car and were off to a country school three miles from Clarinda.

It didn't take us long to reach the school — it never does in Iowa. The consolidation movement has made little headway in this country at least, and there is, in general, a one-room school every two miles. As we entered the room Miss Field was greeted by a battery of smiles from the teacher and the children, who knew her and rejoiced at her coming. She knows by name most of the school children of the county. They also knew how to welcome a stranger, and in a quiet way each endeavored to show me a thoughtful attention. I was soon decorated with the Page County badge — an enamelled clover leaf bearing three H's and the words "Page County, Iowa." The spirit that pervaded the school made it easy to guess what the H's stood for — "head," "hand," and "heart."

In the school room I immediately perceived a wholesome country atmosphere that characterized all the schools we visited. Many of the boys were dressed in "jumpers" and they wore them proudly as a uniform of a most honorable calling. In addition to the maps, globes, and other equipment of the ordinary school there were tables and seed testing boxes made by the boys with ordinary farm tools, while collections of seeds and exhibits of insects were displayed on the walls. The composition book of one grade was entitled, "Things we should know about home," and the index showed such subjects as, "Why I like to live in the country," "How to make a loaf of bread," "How to make a bed," "How to use the Babcock milk tester." A grammar lesson was in progress. Even in this formal subject there appeared many applications of Miss Field's motto: "We must teach a country child in terms of country life." The boy who was called on to illustrate a compound sentence did not struggle vainly to remember some sentence which he had seen in the book or had read in ancient history, but, looking quite naturally out of the school window on a neighboring orchard, said, "It is the 9th of October, and the farmers are gathering apples."

At the close of the school I was honored with a special introduction to the girl who took the prize for the best cookies at the last industrial fair, to the boy who had taken the prize for the best ear of corn, and to the school representative in the industrial fair organization, with whom Miss Field held a brief consultation about the next school exhibit.

In the meantime the children who had been dismissed were waiting outside the school room on the lawn for Miss Field and the game that she had promised to

teach them at her next visit. The next ten minutes on the well-kept lawn cemented more closely the friendships of the school room and left each child richer in social possibilities.

On the way back to Clarinda, Miss Field stated briefly her educational principles and her methods of work as county superintendent.

When she entered the office, the schools of Page County were little better or worse than the ordinary country system in Iowa. The teachers were, for the most part, without special training and there was little professional enthusiasm. It was no unusual thing to change positions at the end of each school term of two or three months. Most of the country pupils dropped out of school at the end of the period of compulsory attendance, and only about fifty per year completed the eighth grade. The teachers taught reading, writing, arithmetic, and the other elementary subjects in the ordinary, conventional way. Hence they believed that, if you developed a boy's general intelligence by means of parsing, he would instinctively know how to select a milch cow or how to organize a coöperative fruit grower's association; or if he learned about the German Empire thoroughly, he would in some way develop later into a good corn grower or an enthusiastic poultry breeder; or if he learned to solve problems in cube root, he would of course know how to estimate the capacity of a corn crib or test a sample of milk for the percentage of butter-fat. They assumed that if a pupil worked hard enough on the ideas and ideals connected with the history of Egypt, he would thereby eventually develop a patriotic devotion to Page County.

Miss Field adopted a very simple philosophy. It was this: "If mental discipline acquired in one field of study spreads over the border and enables the student to work better in another, why shouldn't we begin with the actual life of Page County and spread out from there? Instead of trying to teach a love for the whole United States in general and trusting that in some mysterious way this will eventually percolate down to the school district, why not aim to develop an intense love for the school and a loyalty to Page County and let this gradually expand into a larger patriotism?"

Miss Field's philosophy has worked. Her first task was to inspire and train her teaching force. As she visited the schools of the county she picked out from the 130 teachers a dozen who were willing to meet regularly and led them to organize themselves into a Progressive Teachers' Club. These began a systematic study of the specific rural school problems of the county and made a steady effort to relate their schools vitally to the life of the community. Certain definite things to be done by the teachers were fixed as prerequisites to admission to the organization, and one by one the other teachers applied for membership and were received until now every teacher in the county is a member of the Progressive Club. Few of these teachers are college or normal school graduates. Most have received their professional training as the result of their experience under Miss Field's supervision, in the discussions of the Progressive Club, in the county institute, or in the summer session of the state normal school. Thirty-five teachers from the county attended the state summer school during the past summer. The county institute is held for ten days during the summer. I asked Miss Field if attendance at the institute were compulsory. She replied that it was purely voluntary. "How many of your teachers attend?" I asked. "They were all there," she answered, as if it were a matter of course.

Miss Field is a sincere friend to all her teachers, and they are loyal to her accordingly. The salary schedule in Page County is higher than the average in Iowa. Miss Field's own example is a continuous lesson in appreciation, and the school patrons have not been slow to learn to express their appreciation in those ways which mean quite as much as money to the conscientious worker.

The ideals for the year are set before the teachers in a list of questions on school progress that is sent out early and that is returned at the close of the school term. The blank contains such questions as these:

Has your school year been lengthened? Are the teachers' wages higher than last year? Have the number of classes on the programme been lessened? How many attendance certificates have you issued? How many diplomas and pins? Have the older pupils remained through the school year? Can your school sing "Iowa"? Did your school take any part in the county essay contest? In the county boys and girls' industrial exposition and corn show? Are there boys and girls in your district enrolled in the state junior agricultural work? Have you taught the farm arithmetic work? What have you done in manual training and hand work? State anything else that you have done to connect your school more closely with the farms and homes in your district and to serve their interests. Have you a school garden? State all that has been done to make the school house and grounds more beautiful and useful. Are your pupils thoughtful and courteous? Is there improvement in habits of study? Has your school done anything for your district in the way of literary societies and social recreations?

We may easily imagine the effect of such definite and concrete ideals set before the teachers.

Early next morning I found Miss Field in her office with her secretary, opening the day's mail. Many of the letters were from members of her student coöperative committee, which has a representative in every school. They were in response to inquiries from Miss Field concerning the pupils of the district who had not yet started to school. She finds the student committee one of her strongest helpers in the county organization. On display in the office were the state trophies that had been won by the schools of the county.

We were soon in the car again and on our way to the Olive Branch school. Although the morning was inclement most of the pupils were on hand. We arrived for the opening exercise. Among the songs were "Iowa" and "The Whistling Farmer Boy."

The morning nature lesson was a

recognition and discussion of weeds that had been gathered on the way to school, and a drill on the recognition of the varieties of apples that were being harvested in the community. It was October 10th, the day on which seed corn is selected in Iowa. A pupil gave the reasons for picking seed corn at that time, and two boys with a string exemplified the best way to hang up the corn after it has been selected. The primary reading lesson that followed was based on a chart that had been made by the teacher in which she had used the pictures of birds common in the community, with sentences about the appearance and habits of each. ·

The arithmetic class was studying mensuration. The pupils had each been told to measure a corn crib at home, and the problems that were given them to work at the board had to do with the capacity of the crib, the amount of corn that it would hold, and the value of the corn. For the guidance of her teachers and pupils along practical lines, Miss Field has written a farm arithmetic, that she calls "a book of real problems for farm boys and girls," and which she says "contains nothing about longitude or time, cube root, English money, or the binomial theorem, but is devoted to the sort of work that the farm boys and girls will use every day in actual life."

The manual training work for the boys displayed in the school room was related to the practical work of the farm, and included such pieces as kitchen tables, milk stools, and models for farm devices that had been made during the year.

This same common-sense adaptation of the conventional course of study to the needs of every day life characterized all the schools we visited. Not that the knowledge of the pupils is confined to local material, but in their contemplation of the distant Italy beyond the Alps they habitually recognize the solid earth of Page County beneath their feet.

Miss Field has not found it desirable to develop extensive school gardens. The school grounds are covered with bluegrass, are well-kept, and are usually ornamented with beds of tulips and other simple flowers. The dominant motive in Page County is to centre in the home the larger part of the pupil's activity. The summer holiday prevents a full development of the school garden, and the work at home under the inspiration of the school enlists a more active interest on the part of the parents.

The motive for the manual and industrial work is furnished by the county industrial fair that is held every December. At this fair prizes are offered by the business men of the county for all kinds of handiwork, and the boys and girls of the county are busy months in advance preparing for it. The county superintendent of education and the teachers furnish the suggestions, directions, and the inspiration for this work, and the pupils do it mostly at home. As we rode over the county Miss Field pointed out the home where the boy lived who had taken first prize on his acre yield, or where the girl lived who had been a member of the cooking team that had won the state trophy at Ames.

Occasionally we came to a section of the road that was very much better than other sections over which we had passed. Miss Field explained that one prize at the industrial fair was given for the best model of the King road drag, and that the automobile association had offered a prize to the Page County boy who, with a road drag, would keep a half mile of road in the best condition. She pointed out the home of a boy who had been thought incorrigible, but who had been changed into one of the most reliable boys in the county through the activity and interest that had been aroused by participation in a corn raising and corn judging contest.

She told how handy farm devices, model kitchens, and devices for lightening the labor in the home are becoming universal in the county through the influence of the models exhibited in the school contests at the industrial fair; how prizes offered for miniature model farms, showing the placing of house, barns, orchard, pasture, and giving a crop rotation plan for five years, had resulted not only in a creditable exhibit but also in a universal knowledge of the best crop rotations for the county.

Entry in the industrial fair may be made

by the individual boys and girls or by the school. A silver trophy is awarded to the school making the best exhibit. The child who does not win in these contests is not forgotten, and every exhibitor is presented with the clover leaf pin of Page County.

For the last two years a specialty of the agricultural and industrial work has been the boys' farm camp. This is held for two weeks in connection with the Chautauqua Assembly at Clarinda. Prof. E. C. Bishop, formerly state superintendent of schools for Nebraska, but now in charge of the extension work at Ames, has charge of the camp and directs the games and sports of the boys. Prof. R. K. Bliss and Prof. Murl McDonald of Ames offer short courses in stock judging and in corn and grain judging. From the boys who take this course, teams are selected and sent to take the agricultural short course offered at the state college of agriculture in January. The Page County team has won the state trophy in corn judging for two years in succession, and hopes next January to win it for the third time and thus to keep it permanently. The boys who go to Ames come back to the county and help teach the younger boys who will later hold up the banner of Page County.

The boys' camp was such a success that the people thought they must have a camp for the girls also. They called it "The Camp of the Golden Maids." The girls at the camp study cooking and sewing under Mrs. Knowles and Miss Campbell of the state college. The county cooking team was selected and sent to the state college for the short course, and, as you may easily guess, brought home the state cooking trophy which now keeps company with the other trophies in the county superintendent's office.

All this work has resulted in a Page county school spirit that is almost invincible. One noteworthy result of the new educational spirit is the almost total elimination of the school discipline problem. The boys and girls are too busy for mischief, and the teachers are too busy and interested to indulge in those morbid mental states that make school management difficult.

At the close of the school session every spring, graduating exercises are held at convenient points in the county, and those who have finished the course in the elementary schools meet and, in the presence of parents and friends, are awarded the county certificate.

Two years ago the Omaha Exposition offered an automobile as a prize to the county whose schools would send the best agricultural and industrial exhibit. Page county won. What should be done with the automobile? "Why, give it to Miss Field, of course, so that she can come to see us oftener," was the answer in one voice. Miss Field has the automobile yet, and almost every day in Page County you may meet her out among the county schools, an inspiration to all who come in contact with her.

TWENTY YEARS OF FEMALE SUFFRAGE

This interesting discussion relates the background of **suffrage** for women, the legislation involved, voting patterns, and the role of women in office.

IDAHO'S TWENTY YEARS OF WOMAN SUFFRAGE

By Pearl Tyer

President Boisé Chapter, Nation Council of Women Voters

Twenty years of "votes for women" in actual practice should be able to give a satisfactory answer to the question of its advisability. Idaho is a State rounding out this experience, and a careful survey of the status of its civic affairs and the effects of its equal suffrage may contain important information.

EFFECT DISCERNED IN TREND OF STATE

Its effect can best be discerned in the trend of the civic development of the State itself, for Idaho was not established with set institutions nor convictions before suffrage was a factor. Admission as a State was granted in 1890, and six years later, in November, 1896, the suffrage amendment was passed at the general election and the ballot became a reserve power back of the influence of women. In the early years of Statehood Idaho was a rough-and-ready land with sparse settlements and few railways. The first settlers were gold-seekers, prospecting a bit on their way to California; then, following, came a hardy few who sought new homes because the fire of adventure was in them. The destruction of the Civil War drove others to this almost unknown land. Although the early stories of Idaho do not partake of the reckless disregard of human life incident to some pioneer communities, it was not until the general exodus to the Far West brought hundreds of citizens, ambitious and abounding in energy, that it began its great change in civic ideals.

Woman suffrage cannot claim the entire credit for this change from the free and open days if the saloon and gambling tables, but woman suffrage became alive at the time the change began and was one of the factors. Two years after Idaho became a State, at the Republican State Convention, several of the prominent office-holders were intoxicated in public. This was a period in the history of prohibition when the Republican party in some of the

older States was passing prohibition enactments. The
spectacle of drunkenness was so disgusting to one of the
delegates, now a distinguished citizen, that he determined upon a woman suffrage policy as the surest remedy.
Two years later he was one of the most arduous workers
in the campaign for suffrage which was indorsed at the
conventions of all three parties. This citizen claims
that this was the turning-point for State-wide prohibition, which reached its goal last January, when every
saloon was closed by statutory enactment.

INFLUENCE OF WOMEN'S VOTES NOTICEABLE
IMMEDIATELY

The influence of woman suffrage was noticeable immediately upon the passage of the amendment. H. E.
McElroy, a prominent attorney and candidate for Governor
on the Progressive ticket in 1914, wrote at the time the
women cast their first ballot: "It was tacitly understood
among politicians that the standard must be raised in
order to avoid scratching by the new voters. In fact,
the expectation is universal, for some cause or other,
that women will make independent voters, and party names
will not save undeserving candidates."
James H. Hawley, afterward Governor of Idaho, said
of the first election in which women participated: "The
ladies turned out very generally on the day of election,
and were everywhere treated with the greatest respect, and
never in my experience have I seen a more orderly election. The very presence of the ladies at the polls
seemed to entirely eliminate many of the objectionable
features of former elections."

MEN AND WOMEN COMRADES

Naturalness is an expressive word for the manner in
which women exercise their citizenship in a State which
has developed under the suffrage regime. Men and women
are comrades in civic endeavor. The condition of sex
organization based upon sex, and not upon the general
obligation of citizenship borne by all, to which Charles
E. Hughes has recently called attention, will be found
to be a condition preceding woman suffrage and not ac-
companying it. The privilege of the ballot for twenty
years in Idaho has broadened woman's outlook, and pride
in sex accomplishment has correspondingly lessened. To
designate an institution or legal enactment as men's or
women's is as difficult as to dissociate the father's
and mother's influence in a harmonious household. Some
measures are mothered especially by a woman's organization, but all such have their champions among the men,
and women work together for their adoption. The term,
women's measures, is an anomaly both as to purpose and

history.

LEGISLATION

The catalogue of measures which have been presented
to the legislature under the tutelage of women, either
individually or representing women's clubs, and which
were persistently cared for until finally signed by the
Governor as a statue, includes a public library commission and library control (there were previously no library provisions), child labor prohibition and juvenile
court creation, humane society, equal property rights for
men and women, equal custody of children, right of women
to make their own wills, the Iowa Infringement and A-
batement Law, making wife desertion an extraditable misdemeanor, pensions for mothers, nine-hour law for women,
State Industrial School, Institution for Feeble-Minded,
separate dormitory for women at State University, placing
domestic science in the University, and appropriation
for Children's Home-Finding Society. The only legislative measure which women have worked for at more than
one Legislature and lost is the Civil Service Bill.
Yet this phenomenal legislative record has been accomplished in the Legislatures of twenty years, in which
but three women were seated. This illustrates the co-
operation of the men and women. In every "women's measure" the genius of men and women has united.

Although to a large extent intuitively and uncon-
sciously, in their legislative methods women have been
fulfilling the essential requisites of lawmaking in a dem-
ocracy. It is fundamentally true under a representative
form of government that the power is with the people and
not the legislators. The conception of legislation in a
republic is that the demand should be with the consent
of the governed and should come from the people up to the
lawmaking body, and not be induced from the lawmaking
body down to the people.

Women's part in lawmaking has included the education
of public sentiment to seek the desired measure. By
educating themselves through the women's organizations,
which are largely the instruments through which such
public opinion takes form, and by agitating the proposition and keeping it as a reminder in the press, the
desired reforms have come in naturally and quietly. The
statutes providing for a commission form of government
for cities, a direct primary law, the discretionary
power of judges, and the labor of convicts on State improvements outside the penitentiary walls are examples
of measures which were thoroughly discussed in women's
meetings and reported in the press, but which were not
introduced by them in the Legislature. The anti-gambling
law was passed shortly after the ballot was granted to
women and before the State Federation of Clubs was or-

ganized. William Balderston, editor of the Idaho "Daily
    Statesman," at that time wrote:
    "The influence of this new voting element was felt
in the Legislature in the passage of the law prohibiting
gambling. It is universally conceded that such an Act
could not have been passed had it not been for the fact
that the members felt they would be held to account by
that portion of the population which is unalterably opposed to the vice that ruins such large numbers of men.
It is a significant fact that the law was passed without
any organized movement on the part of the women. It
was the silent influence of woman as a voter that carried it through."
    The State Federation of Women's Clubs, which is the
most prominent women's organization legislatively, does
not seek the enactment of a measure which has not had
at least a year of State-wide discussion and propaganda.
The Woman's Christian Temperance Union also has always
depended upon the education of the masses rather than
upon "lobbying" its bills through.

WOMEN'S ATTITUDE TO OFFICE-SEEKERS

    Idaho women, with meager exceptions, are not poli-
ticians. They are not to be found where political trick-
ery and trading are in practice. They work by fostering
certain measures and by doing their part in the election
of officials who will uphold these measures. Sometimes
a mass-meeting is called at the instigation of the women,
and candidates for office are called upon before election
to state their attitude on certain points. The Boisé
Council of Women Voters, in union with the Good Citizenship Club, which had experienced difficulty in securing
certain park actions in Boisé, before the next city
election invited the nominees for mayor and commissioners
to appear before them and express their views on parks
and playgrounds. Not one of the candidates apparently
considered the meeting unimportant. Ten were present,
and the remaining two, who were unable to be present,
sent written statements. The sentiments of the candidates were given to the public through the press. The
Legislative Committee of the State Federation of Women's
Clubs secures the attitude of all candidates for the
Legislature before the election upon the measures which
they propose to present at that session. When the le-
gislator come to the capital, he is sometimes confronted
by his own written statement of his pre-election views.
    Should an official fail to keep his promise to a
woman's organization, he is advertised throughout his
territory and told that he will not be further supported.
These "clearings up" have been without demonstrations of
malice and universally accomplished with dignity. The
most notable example of the politician disappointing

women and the reforming is Herman H. Taylor, Lieutenant-
Governor. He came to the legislature in 1912 as President of the Senate with a plurality of 6,403 votes.
During this session he used his influence ahainst the
measures offered by the women, to which he had been
thought favorable. In the election of 1914 his plurality was reduced to 464. At the Susan B. Anthony banquet
that year he acknowledged publicly that the women had almost defeated him; during that Legislature he supported
the measures which had been defeated largely through
him the previous session. Washington County is a strong
woman's club center; in 1912 it sent a Representative
to the Legislature pledged to support the Iowa Injunction
and Abatement Law for the closing of houses of bad re-
pute; he became its opponent and was chairman of the
committee in which it died. He was defeated for re-
election to the next session, at which the bill was almost unanimously passed.

WOMEN IN OFFICE

The women themselves are not largely office-seekers.
On the ballot the only offices commonly containing their
names are those of State Superintendent of Public Instruction and Treasurer, and county superintendents,
treasurers, and members of the Legislature. The office
of State Superintendent has been occupied by women for
the past sixteen years, and that of State Librarian
since its creation. Three-fourths of the county superintendents are women, and one-third of the treasurers.
The clerkships and second deputyships held by women in
State offices and the number of women employed in State
institutions bring more than half of the State pay-roll
to women.

The presence of women in caucuses and political
gatherings is kindly met by the men. This condition is
also true in the neighboring State of Utah, as is illustrated by the following incident: A prominent Utah woman was being told the story of an Idaho woman's attendance as a delegate at the Republican State Convention,
and was told that when the Idaho woman had mentioned this
fact to a Far Eastern woman the Eastern woman had exclaimed, enthusiastically, "Oh, and did the women send
you?" The Utah resident interrupted the story at this
point. "No, the men sent her," she said. A man had
placed the Idaho woman's name in nomination and another
had resigned his place in her favor.

NON-PARTISANSHIP

Party lines are not held as closely by the women as
by the men, which may account for the adoption of a
State primary law and the commission form of government

in Boisé, both of which eliminate the old-time party
conventions with their trading and machine rule. The
women compose part of the membership of the Hughes-Fair-
banks Clubs now under State organization, and two years
ago there was a woman's Democratic Club; but the organi -
zations where the women work shoulder to shoulder for
civic reforms, as the Good Citizen Club, the Council of
Women Voters, and civic departments of literary clubs,
are invariably non-partisan. The measures thus launched
are generally indorsed by all political parties or their
candidates. The recent prohibition law, springing from
the Women's Christian Temperance Union and the Anti-Sa-
loon League was placed in the platform of both political
parties and passed the Legislature with but one dissen-
ting vote. The policy of making a measure an issue in
one party and asking the women to vote outside their
party to support it has never been followed.

Non partisanship in lawmaking by both men and women
is shown in the activity of the Legislative League,
which was in session during the last session of the
legislature. This was organized by men engaged in various branches of business, and included in its membership
by their invitation business women and representatives
of every woman's civic club. The purpose was to study
measures under debate in the Legislature with the aim
of encouraging good and hindering immature and hasty
enactment; insurance men, commission merchants, attorneys, Mothers' Congress delegates, and Federation Club
workers co-operated with the Legislature and gave them
the advantage of the more extensive view-point.

MEN MORE FAMILIAR WITH CIVIL
GOVERNMENT

Although the Western-trained woman takes her balloting naturally, the race training which for generations
has endowed men with this responsibility is noticeable
in the greater familiarity of the men with statutory
technicalities. As yet the conversation and companion-
ships of the average girl do not give her as accurate a
civic training as her brother's although she is intelli-
gently informed. Mrs. Cynthia Mann, a teacher at the
time of the adoption of suffrage, and later donor of the
Idaho State Children's Home site, said in a memorandum
the year following suffrage:
"Another effect that is worthy of notice is the great
interest among the pupils of our public schools in the
study of political economy. The girls often felt less
interest in this science because they would have no voice
in political affairs, while most boys said that they
could vote without studying this science. Now the girls,
like their mothers look upon this new responsibility
as a grave one. The boys are not to be outdone, and it

is delightful to see the zeal with which they attack this
so-called dull study."

The average woman grown to maturity in a non-suffrage
State in removing to a suffrage State accepts her new
privilege as a burden, while it is probable that the
daughter is abounding in the joy of having a part with
her father and brothers in the local affairs. But when
a question up for election appeals to the mother as one
of right or wrong, the voting ceases to be a burden and
becomes a weapon.

The training received as clerks and judges of election is valuable to the women. An Illinois judge has
made mention of the efficient clerical work of the women
in the elections of Chicago recently, upon which new
labor the women of that State are entering. The greater
part of the book work in connection with elections in
Idaho, including registration and polling, is done by
the women, which gives them a more intimate conception
of the machinery of government. The polls are quiet and
maintain somewhat the dignity of a formal social function
with men and women present.

The omens are already in the sky predicting that women may become more informed as citizens than the men.
The women's clubs for civic study and the practical
application which is given their balloting are having
a broadening and educational effect. Where is to be
found an organization of men with the purpose of per-
fecting the members for the more efficient performance
of the duties of citizenship? The history of education,
which at first in the annals of mankind was restricted
to the masculine sex, may be considered as a precedent,
the number of women completing high school and collegiate
courses now exceeding that of the men.

IS THE FEMININITY OF WOMEN AFFECTED?

Has the ballot affected the femininity of women? If
the charm of womanhood has escaped with the entrance of
the ballot, both men and women are so blind to the condition as not to know their loss. Rare indeed would be
the person found repining for the good old days when
women couldn't vote. Do the women vote the same as their
husbands? Some women vote to the dication of the men,
which condition will continue until every woman knows
how to express her own self. The point is, the woman
who is awake to her privilege of expression has it, and
is potentially possible to the unknowing one when she
awakens. Some men still sleep. There has not been a
record of the percentage of men and women voting, but
in some precincts it is said that more women than men
vote.

THE OLD AND NEW IDEALS OF CITIZENSHIP

Twenty years of the ballot in the hands of women
with men in Idaho has developed the State along moral
and advanced lines, with legislation which has outrun
the old Puritanical States of their forefathers. The
temptations of the early days--drink, gambling, and
houses of ill repute--are swept away. But it is claimed
by some who have watched the change of the past twenty-
five years that Idaho with statutes, granting them en-
forced, is not as righteous as Idaho without statutes.
The story of the pack-driver with one barrel of whisky
more than he could haul up the hill is told to illustrate the former integrity. Finding it impossible to
continue his journey so heavily loaded, the driver deposited the barrel of drink by the roadside with two
cups, one for the passing travelers to partake of the
contents and the other to receive the pay. Later he
returned and took his cup of coin. No such sense of
honor is universal to-day, say the story-tellers. Yet
even they would hardly want to go back to the old days.

SUFFRAGE SANE IN ITS OPERATION

The intense attitude of some of the promoters of
equal suffrage might have led to the belief that when
the reform went into operation the commonwealth would
be in a state of upheaval and that radical measures
would be enacted to the disturbance of the common peace.
Its practice, however, has proved that it does not
carry a destructive tendency. Eighteen months after its
adoption Mrs. Cynthia Mann, quoted above, wrote:
"When the Supreme Court of Idaho decided that the
equal suffrage amendment had carried, it was pleasing
to note how quickly all aggressive opposition ceased.
Those who had been zealous opponents refrained from
predicting the evil consequences that would be the result of women voting, and at all elections held since,
primary, municipal, and school, have vied with the ardent advocates of this reform in politics in securing
the presence at the polls of this new element in governmental affairs."
It has continued sane in its operation; the leaders
among the women are of a high type. Its inherent policy
of educating the general public to its reforms burns out
fanaticism in the long journey of the proposed enactments through committees, local discussions, and press
reports. The exaggeration of energy displayed in the
fray for suffrage is one of the results of antagonism.
When the antagonism is withdrawn and suffrage is permitted to fill its mission, its course has been found
to be orderly and constructive. This is the inevitable
working of the metaphysical law. For equal suffrage

is an expression of the principle of equality, and, as a principle in operation, can produce only harmony and satisfaction in its proper manifestation.

A COUNTRY READY FOR CAPITAL

The state of Idaho offered numerous opportunities
for investment of capital. The following article
describes the possibilities for investment and the various
industries now in operation.

A COUNTRY READY FOR CAPITAL

**GREAT DISTRICTS THAT HAVE BEEN OPENED BUT NOT DEVEL-
OPED -- THE BEGINNING OF A FLOW OF EASTERN MONEY**

BY

C. M. K.

DOWN in a bend of the Clearwater Mountains, under the shadow of Mount Idaho, there is a little city called Grangeville. Around it stretch the prairies — rich, rolling, verdant. In the spring, its roads and streets are knee-deep in black volcanic mud. In the summer, dust flies in clouds.

Forty-five years ago, men planted Grangeville — men of strong faith, and courage beyond the understanding of civilized people. Since that day, many tides have swept about it. Pierce City and Buffalo Hump, reckless camps of miners, sprung up in the mountains behind it, lived their uproarious day, then faded into history. The worst of Montana, fleeing the vigilantes, came down through the Nez Perces and Lolo passes, and made the place a one-night stand on the road to Lewiston. Floods of people came and went, miners, farmers, drovers, stockmen, timber cruisers bound for the hills, traders bound coastwise — everyone came, and most went.

A few stayed. A cattleman, saving hard-earned money, laid it out in a farm on the blue-flowered prairie. A sheep-tender came and settled beside him. The little store, as time went on, grew bigger, trading with passing miners, prospectors, and farm-hunters. Then, as the mining camps in the hills multiplied, trade grew rapidly — and the town struck its roots deeper into the prairie and announced that it was there to stay.

Now it is the county seat of Idaho County, which is as big as Rhode Island, Delaware, and Massachusetts put together. Grangeville's population is about four thousand people. It has banks, electric lights, good stores. In May it was talking about macadamized streets, and a trolley line that struggles fitfully along the prairie.

There is nothing flashy or wonderful about Grangeville. It looks as though it took hard work to make it — and would take more hard work to make it very big. Yet, as solid as its foundation is, the town lives on the conquest of the country, not on its development; for there has been no real development. A typical Grangeville citizen will tell you, for example, that he herded cattle in the ridges forty years ago. Then he planted wheat on the prairie, and fed it to hogs so that it could walk to market by itself. Then, when the railroad came to Stites, twenty odd miles away, he grew rich hauling wheat to the railroad by wagon. Two years ago, the railroad came up Lapwai Cañon, and he grew richer, selling wheat to a great grain-buying company, right on the ranch.

And so with all of them. There is nothing very grand or picturesque about them — but they have laid the foundations for the development of the country. They have not amassed any mighty fortunes buying irrigable lands at

$100 an acre and selling the same at $2,000; nor in fliers in mines or standing timber; but they have made fifty bushels of wheat grow to the acre where only bunch grass and the blue-flowered camas grew before.

Grangeville is a part of the old West. You will not see it from a Pullman window. You will have to get off at Spokane, or Boise, or Lewiston, and travel by branch line or stage for half a day before you reach its fringes.

And with the present generation it may be that it will disappear entirely. Still, in the breaks of the Idaho rivers and out along the dry upland benches, the cattlemen carry guns, wear chaps and sombreros, and talk the same old lingo — but they are few and far between, and perfectly harmless. They and the sheep-herders, uncanny people, are still the dominant inhabitants of Mr. Harriman's Central Oregon; but even there the time grows short, and they all know it.

"It's gittin' time," said one in the Nez Perces Cañon, "fer me to git. Fer civilization 'll wipe me out sure as consumption gits the Injuns."

It is all getting crowded back into pretty small corners, this old West. Now, there lies on the table this morning's copy of the *Portland Oregonian*. A front-page story tells of surveying parties, representing Mr. Harriman and the Milwaukee road, locating lines through the Lolo Pass. They have been doing that for years; but some day someone will really come through Lolo Pass, just as, some time, somebody will shove a railroad through every rift in the mountain chain. And when it happens the West will move again. Elk City, to-day almost a Bret Harte camp, only a little more sordid at heart, a little tougher inside and better upholstered outside, will be tamed to look like Cripple Creek, or Wallace, or any other mining centre on the main lines. Grangeville, Idaho — and all the other Grangevilles that men made grow in hard places — will cease to be Grangeville when it listens to the thunder of the transcontinentals through the mountain passes.

Just across the Clearwater Cañon from the Camas and Nez Perces prairies lies another wonderful stretch of farm land. They call it by its Indian name, the Palouse. It, too, has been farmed for many years, but such farming! The land is rich beyond all measure.

"If you leave it alone," said a Moscow man, "a house and barn would grow the first year; and a piano and automobile might be looked for the second."

The farmers, from an Eastern point of view, do leave it alone sure enough; and there are many automobiles and pianos in the Palouse townships; so the statement is not so bad as it looks. There is no fertilizing, no irrigation, little cultivation, no dairying, hardly any stock, nothing but grain and hay for market. The ranches are enormous; the profits immense. In the winter, there is nothing to do; so the farmers go to California, Japan, or Florida. A good many have quit farming altogether, renting the farms on shares. A few each year sell out, and put their money out on mortgages at 40 per cent. of the value of the farms. They get 8 per cent. and 10 per cent. in normal times; and more at other times.

In the East the farmer's wife is in the habit of selling butter and eggs and chickens to the stores in country towns, and buying groceries, clothes, etc. with the proceeds. In Lewiston, the farmers' wives come into town, sometimes in automobiles, and buy at retail cold storage eggs, butter made in creameries, chickens raised in town, and often strawberries and other luxuries out of season.

The produce markets of many small towns are supported by the buying of the farmers and their families.

In this area there seem to be no dairy herds, or fancy stock of any sort. In the fruit regions of western Washington, one may see herds of Jersey cows, and wonderful horses — but in the Palouse the people pay no attention to cattle, and the stock looks scrubby. Even the hogs are just plain hogs.

As time goes on, they are going to get over this sort of thing and begin to farm. One may travel for miles through the rolling hills of the Palouse to-day, and hardly see a single farmhouse. Every foot of it is handled, yet in a school section seven miles long and four miles wide there are less than forty children. And down in the Tammany Country, so-called, half a dozen men own, and farm, an area that produces from seven hundred thousand to one million bushels of wheat a year.

In this inland empire, there are probably more undeveloped opportunities than in any other equal area in the world. One cannot read the facts, as gathered by the state offices of Idaho and Washington without realizing that here are honest fortunes going to waste.

In a single year, for instance, Idaho imported 900,000 cases of canned goods, tomatoes, fruit, corn, peas, etc. Yet all these products grow in profusion in Idaho — and there was not, at that time, a single cannery in the state!

In the same year, more than 10,000,000 pounds of packing-house products were imported — in spite of the fact that the cattle men of the state sent to the markets 8,624 carloads of cattle, sheep, and hogs.

Every now and again, Idaho and Washington suffer from fuel famines in the winter time; yet the known deposits of coal are limitless. In Fremont County, Idaho, there is coal enough to fill the bunkers of the state and keep them full; but it is only used locally, and not very much at that.

The first cement plant was built in Idaho only two years ago, in spite of the fact that an enormous amount of concrete has been used annually for several years in the building of dams and bridges. Recently, there has been great activity in this line, the industry springing up here and there, backed by small capital, but apparently very healthy in its growth.

In Idaho, according to the latest figures, the total amount of capital invested in manufacturing, outside of sawmills, is less than fifteen million dollars. Yet the available water-power, to quote official language, is "sufficient to heat every house, turn every wheel, and illuminate every city in the three Pacific Northwestern states." And anyone who has seen the Snake, the Salmon, the Spokane, and the Payette rivers, will take that to be a very modest boast indeed.

What is true of Idaho is true of eastern Washington, and still more true of Oregon. Above all other things, they need capital — and they need it badly. You could take the State of Massachusetts and lose it bodily in a single county of Idaho; but if 1 per cent. of the capital invested in the next twelve months in Massachusetts industries went into Idaho instead, that state would hum from end to end. That the field is rich nobody doubts — but these great ridges and plains that in their day poured $250,000,000 of gold into the markets of the world go begging to those same markets for capital to open up their more stubborn resources. To the mind of the East, Idaho is still a wild-cat country, as it was in the placer days.

Very slowly indeed, capital turns its eyes upon these Western states. Industry, in years past, has talked against a stone wall of incredulity and indifference, erected by the Eastern capitalist. And it is only in very recent years that the first signs of a change are apparent. The coast country, of course, drew capital first. Boston built the street car and interurban systems of Seattle and Tacoma. New York and Boston are financing an interurban system through the Willamette Valley, ably backed by local Oregon capital.

The inland empire has grown almost alone to what it is to-day. Only very recently, New York bankers joined in the development of the water-power of the Spokane River. Even later another New York bond house underwrote the bonds of an electric railway tapping the wheat lands of the Palouse and the timber wealth of Potlatch. And newer still is the coöperation of a Pittsburgh and a New York firm to carry out an enormous irrigation project in Southern Idaho.

And these are the facts of the greatest significance in the recent records of the far West. It is but a beginning. That its growth will be swift, one may hardly doubt. For example, on the train, I met a Detroit banker, bound for Southwestern Oregon to investigate an irrigation plan. In Spokane, I met a Canadian engineer looking up two projects that may — or may not — be taken up by Toronto capital.

Practically, however, nothing has been done by Oregon, Washington, and Idaho, nor by particular communities, to really attract the attention of pioneer capital in large amounts. So far as I could discover, all the advertising that has been done recently has been directed toward the bringing of people to take up small fruit farms, or wheat lands in quarter sections, or — unhappily — to buy more or less speculative mining stocks. The resources that can be developed by large capital remain untouched, not only in Oregon and Idaho, but even more markedly in Washington and British Columbia.

Timber is the one exception. In the judgment of sane business men in Seattle, Tacoma, and Portland, the timber supply of the Northwestern states will not only make that country rich, but it will furnish the capital that will develop all the other latent resources of the territory.

Roughly, the timber people estimate the

value of the standing timber at about $11,325,000,000. This is on a basis of $15 per 1,000 feet, and puts the amount of standing timber in this area at 755,000,000,000 feet. It is a resource as yet barely touched. According to official figures, not more than one-thirtieth of the merchantable timber, even in Washington, has been marketed. Some of the most powerful capitalists in the United States handle this industry; and a large percentage of the local fortunes in the Northwest have come, directly or indirectly, out of the forests.

There is no doubt that the gradual turning of these giant timber resources into money will ultimately develop all the latent resources of Idaho, Oregon, Washington, and British Columbia. Fifty years ago the greatest lumber state in the Union was Pennsylvania. In a later era it was Michigan. To-day it is the Northwest. And with the forestry methods known now it would be possible to make the forests of these states a great resource for all time. Pennsylvania has practically cut her lumber; and the wealth produced has made her the greatest of manufacturing states. Michigan is becoming every year less a huge lumber camp and more a miscellaneous manufacturing state. The new states, now plundering their forests, may follow the same law, or they may cut their forests carefully and have timber supply still earning for them after the other developments take place. Any one of them might probably claim greater latent resources to-day than Michigan ever had; and collectively they may surpass Pennsylvania.

THE SCENIC MARVELS OF IDAHO

The beautiful scenery found in this part of the
country are described in detail in the following article.

THE SCENIC MARVEL OF IDAHO

THE SNAKE RIVER, A THOUSAND-MILE STREAM, WHICH FLOWS THROUGH
BAD LANDS, OVER A PRECIPICE FIFTY FEET HIGHER THAN NIAGARA, AND
AGAIN AT THE BOTTOM OF A MILE DEEP CANYON—A LAND OF WONDERS

BY

WILLIAM HOWARD KIRKBRIDE

THE world is less familiar with the Snake River of Idaho than with any other river of importance in the United States; and yet it is our seventh largest river—more than a thousand miles long. It is one of the most wonderful and impressive water-ways in the world. The few who have tried to follow its winding course through wild and forbidding extents of lava plateaux, do not wonder that so little is known of it, for no railroads traverse the lifeless desert that borders it, and no boats, for hundred of miles at a stretch, dare ply its waters. It is navigable for only one hundred miles from its junction with the Columbia to the Idaho boundary, and in several isolated sections of the interior. For the greater part of its course it flows through old and magnificent canyons of its own making through desolate and awful wastes, the result of vomiting craters and of convulsions of the earth.

It dashes and roars, in whirlpools and rapids, through forests of mighty pines, between snow-capped peaks, beside extinguished craters, through gloomy chasms, amid an indescribable chaos of weird and fantastic masses of molten rock, crags, peaks, and precipices, through naked deserts; and, again, broad and tranquil, it ripples through smiling meadows, and green, fertile valleys, past prosperous towns and thriving communities,—and is lost again in the deep and solemn canyons.

It rises in the Rocky Mountains, on the southern slope of the Great Divide, and flows southeast, and then west, in a great serpentine curve through Southern Idaho. In the western part of the state it bends sharply northward, and for 250 miles forms the boundary line between Idaho, Oregon, and Washington, and finally empties into the Columbia, twenty miles below the Oregon boundary.

At first it is a mere mountain torrent made up of melted snow from the Teton range. Then for many miles it flows majestically through a silent wilderness of primeval forests, mirroring an endless chain of rugged peaks. Then a great and awful change begins to take place. The deep woods grow assuming the form of a Moorish arch, four hundred yards in width, it takes a precipitous plunge of 190 feet into a smoking abyss below. With a crash and roar that can be heard for miles, the sheet of water hurls itself upon the rocks beneath. Some of it is whipped into threads by the wind, and falls in a never-ending storm of rain-drops.

It can readily be seen, from the number of falls, that the amount of water-power available for irrigation and other purposes is practically unlimited, and yet, owing to the isolated section through which the river passes, its waters have scarcely been utilized. Recently, several extensive irrigation systems, involving much capital, have been established to reclaim the desert wastes of the interior. The success of agriculture in Idaho is dependent, almost entirely, upon irrigation, and, except in those places where the flood plains of the small streams have been cultivated, there is little or no farming. The soil, which is of volcanic-alluvial formation, is fertile, and yields enormous crops when watered. It is safe to assert that the larger portion of South-Central Idaho will some day be one of the most productive districts in America. At a point six miles from Minidoka, the United States Government has built a dam across the Snake, thus raising the river to a height of fifty feet. A large part of the flow is then diverted into channels, from which, by gravity alone, it is distributed over some 65,000 acres of formerly arid land, transforming it into fertile fields and orchards.

At Milner, twenty three miles above Twin Falls, the largest dam in America, and the third largest in the world, has been built by private enterprise. From it run two great canals, one of them to the southwest, sixty-nine miles long, eighty feet wide at the bottom, and 120 feet wide at the top. Two hundred and seventy thousand acres of land have already been made available for cultivation, and several other tracts are soon to be opened.

Aside from the value of the water for irrigation purposes, the power from the many cataracts will some day be utilized. The three great falls afford, at a moderate expense, more than 100,000 horse power, 20,000 horse power of which has already been developed by the Shoshone Falls Power Company at Shoshone Falls.

Beyond the falls, the river is again united in a deep and narrow gorge. Mile after mile the scenery grows wilder, until the spell of the desert, and even the beauty of the falls, is forgotten in the awful grandeur of the canyons. Between the Payette and the Powder Rivers, the Snake flows through one of the most marvelous canyons in the world. The vertical walls of black basalt rise 5,000 feet, and the canyon is so narrow that from the bottom the sky appears as a slender thread of blue. Millions of rocks of every conceivable size and shape, all curiously worn by time and weather, and twisted and gnarled by heat into weird and fantastic forms, hang over the river. Their monstrous shapes are now repulsive, now noble, as they assume the appearance of prison walls or of cathedral towers.

Beyond the Grande Ronde River the canyon walls grow less and less abrupt, and the river, losing much of its ferocity, glides away from its hiding place, and winds in graceful turnings through a broad expanse of prairie and high plateau. The rolling sage-brush plain, though still barren of trees, is no longer dull. Here and there are splashes of color, and the delicate greens of vegetation. Over all rests the desert haze, lending an exquisite less and less dense, the mountains decline into endless rolling hills and deep ravines. At every turn the country grows flatter and more featureless, until a great plain stretches out indefinitely, the gloomy barrenness of which is emphasized by the few pyramid-like cones which stand there, solitary reminders of a dead and terrible period. It is the great Snake River Desert. After an observer's first shock and his feelings of isolation have passed, the boundless plain loses its monotony. The expanse seems to awaken and throb with life, the silent sentinels of the desert tell a tale of long ago, when mysterious forces were at play. For this is the field of the most gigantic volcanic action that ever occurred in America.

Curious evidences of the terrific movements that once took place are apparent at "Cinder Buttes," sixty miles west of Blackfoot, in many well preserved volcanoes of comparatively recent date. The plains are strewn with vast numbers of cinders, bombs, and other volcanic relics.

For 350 miles after passing the Blackfoot

River, which joins the Snake River from the southeast, not a stream reaches it from the north. Many streams rise in the Salmon River Mountains of Central Idaho, all tending toward the Snake River Canyon, but all, sooner or later, are swallowed up in chasms, or are evaporated by the intense heat and dryness of the desert. The "Big Lost," and the "Little Lost," rivers, both of some magnitude, which rise in the mountains and flow in a southerly direction into the Great Desert, vanish there. But after traveling many miles beneath the lava beds of the desert, the pent-up waters break from their bondage into a series of remarkable cataract-springs farther down the river. For twenty miles they gush at intervals from the canyon wall, in ever-flowing streams.

The greatest and the most beautiful is near the town of Hagerman, and is known as Thousand Springs. For a half mile, and from an elevation of from seventy-five to two hundred feet, whole rivers gush forth from the roots of the sage-brush, sometimes in broad white sheets of waving mist, superb in color, like small Niagaras, but more often in a series of tiny falls and glittering cascades, which leap from rock to rock, and finally dissolve in spray as they crash upon the rocks beneath.

The seepage from these lost rivers has wrought other astonishing results in the canyons of the desert. In several places great side alcoves extend northward from the main canyon. These in no way owe their existence to the action of the Snake or other streams. The most noted is the "Lost," or Blue Lake Canyon. It is an immense semi-circular chasm, some two miles long, with perpendicular walls more than 500 feet high. No streams enter from any direction, but at its head and mouth are mammoth springs, discharging many cubic feet of water per second, which have formed two dark blue lakes. The water from these spring-fed lakes, by erosion and by concentration of energy, has eaten its way through solid basalt rock, forming a deep cut canyon.

No other river has as many magnificent cascades and water-falls as the Snake. The greatest is Shoshone Falls. Its volume is less than that of Niagara, but the fall is fifty feet greater, and during the spring flood it is as great a wonder as Niagara. At Idaho Falls, the water throws itself abruptly over a great ridge of basalt rock into a narrow trench below. The American Falls, farther down the river, is even more imposing, for the volume of water is much greater. The Snake broadens before reaching the falls, and then takes a mighty plunge of more than fifty feet. At Salmon Falls, near the mouth of the Big Wood River, the stream dashes, in one cascade, over a declivity thirty feet high. There are many other beautiful falls, all of which would be more or less famous were they not overshadowed by the grandeur of the three cataracts in the south-central part of the state, namely, Shoshone, Auger, and Twin Falls, all within a short distance of each other.

Just before reaching Twin Falls the river is separated by a rugged wall of rock into two turbulent streams of great velocity, which, in the fall of 187 feet, tumble, roaring, into an emerald lake beneath. The waters then rush into another canyon, the walls of which are more than 800 feet high, and din and uproar give place to a deathlike stillness. Before one has had time to grow accustomed to the silence, there comes, up the river, a muffled roar, like approaching thunder. It is the distant booming of Shoshone Falls. Deeper and deeper grows the canyon, until it is a thousand feet deep; wider and wider grows the river until it is a thousand feet wide; louder and louder grows the booming, until it deafens with its loudness. A bend in the river—and there are the falls.

The river rushes down first with a fall of thirty feet, through rocky channels; and then softness and gentleness to the scene. To the north and to the south, the view is bounded by an unbroken chain of snow-capped peaks and crags, which seem to fade into clouds as they join the horizon. Above them all, their snow-burdened summits glistening in the sunlight, loom the spire-like forms of the Seven Devils, abrupt and precipitous peaks. Bold, severe, and forbidding, they tower in their immensity, dwarfing their sister peaks, and making the mild undulations of the desert hills insignificant by comparison.

On nearing the Washington boundary the scenery loses much of its wildness, the narrow canyon walls give way to broad and fertile valleys, the deeply eroded plateaux melt into gently rolling foot-hills, interrupted here and there with belts of waving grain.

When the soil has been made productive by the presence of rivers and streams, thriving villages appear, amid fields of green, pleasing to the eye after the monotonous gray of the lava beds.

Just above the boundary, at the junction of the Snake and Clearwater rivers, there lies a broad and fertile valley, several thousand acres in extent, surrounded by immense foot-hills. Beneath them nestle the twin cities of Lewiston-Clarkston, a prosperous and thriving community. But one watches, with deeper interest, the wonderful hills, that tower 2300 feet above the river, some sharp and jagged, all denuded by erosion, and thrown together in extraordinary irregularity.

At its junction with the Clearwater, the Snake turns sharply westward. The hills again assume the form of rugged perpendicular walls, the river narrows into a turbulent and broken sea-green stream. Nowhere in the Snake River Canyon is there a better example of the columnar basalt formation than here. In many instances the lava, on cooling, has retained a perpendicular position in the form of columns and pillars, sometimes huge and massive, like the ruins of a Roman temple, but more often in graceful, symmetrical sheets, even and delicately wrought.

For another hundred miles the Snake flows westward through its canyon, until, twenty miles below its Oregon boundary, after a lonely course of 1050 miles, it pours into the mighty Columbia.

HOW IDAHO GOT PURE FOOD

This discussion illustrates the problems faced by all parts of the nation, as well as Idaho, in maintaining proper food standards and cooking conditions.

World's Work, March, 1914.

HOW IDAHO GOT PURE FOOD
BY
ISAAC RUSSELL

IN IDAHO every Pullman porter carries on a swat-the-fly crusade and two electric fans play upon the cook in the dining-car kitchen so that the food may be free from the sweat of his toil. In that state Federal judges have ordered all the prisoners removed from certain jails and the bedding in the condemned jails burned up to the last pillow-case, the shame of maintaining such a prison being so well advertised in the meantime that the people tore it down and commenced forthwith to build a new one in strict conformity with the best ideas on sanitation possessed by the voting women of the neighborhood.

These are some of the works of Sanitary Inspector James H. Wallis, who has also carried new sanitary standards into the drug stores, the eating-houses, the big corporations, the canneries, the slaughter houses, and even the public schools.

Mr. Wallis first met the problem of railroad dining cars on a trip from his home town — which, on account of his swat-the-fly crusade there, has taken on the sobriquet of "Buzzless Boise" — to Salt Lake City, in the neighboring state of Utah.

Tainted chops were served to a merchant of Glenns Ferry, Idaho. He was paying a fancy price for them and up to that moment had never suspected that tainted meat would be served in such luxurious surroundings as prevail on the usual dining car. A newspaper man, on the same train, told Mr. Wallis. Mr. Wallis made no disturbance with the waiters but he went to the kitchen. There he showed his badge and announced that he intended to make an inspection.

He found, first, that the cook was working in a hot little compartment without ventilation. Next he noticed that flies filled the compartment, attracted doubtless by the rancid smell of bad meat. In the ice boxes he found bad chops, slimy steaks, decaying vegetables. He asked kindly questions of the cook about the reason for it all, and learned that his particular dining car was on the home stretch of a long run out of Ogden, Utah, to Huntington, Ore. The custom, he found, was to stock the car in Ogden and not to restock it again until its return. More than that, there were credit marks for the dining car conductor who served his goods so sparingly that he always carried the largest amount of surplus. Mr. Wallis took note of the surprising amount of perspiration on the brow of the cook and also of the frying pans into which it fell. He made a second inspection late at night and noticed the feet of husky Negro waiters protruding from blankets laid down over the dining car tables. Next day he searched for the blankets and found them — stowed away on shelves in the pantry above packages of food that the cook had left open!

Mr. Wallis's manners are the mildest in the world. Neither cook nor waiter nor dining-car conductor even guessed that he was shocked and indignant. Instead of making a display of anger he was thinking out a way to clinch the legal evidence should he be called upon in court to prove what he had seen. He went back to his own car, solicited the help of some friends he found there, and had them look over the whole situation with him.

Then, gently, he approached the dining-car conductor. He received some rather heated suggestions that his jurisdiction was on the other side of a state boundary line some distance to the north.

"All right," he said softly, "I am sorry you look at it that way because I would have preferred to settle this matter quietly without bringing scandal upon the railroad. But I shall now be compelled to exercise that jurisdiction of which you spoke in my own territory."

PUBLICITY AS A POLICEMAN

Now Mr. Wallis had been a newspaper proprietor and he had learned how to make a story into "news." He knew also that there was no policeman so good as the light, properly turned on. So in a few days he had the newspapers handle the story. Mr. Wallis seized all the food, good, bad, and indifferent, in the dining-car lockers.

"But it's perfectly good food," protested the dining-car conductor.

"But it wouldn't be perfectly good food by the time it reached passengers traveling on your road in this state," replied Mr. Wallis. "How could it be," he added, "when it is carried on the cars so long, and there is no ventilation in the kitchen and it is bound to be cooked with a liberal sprinkling of perspiration?"

The officials began to protest loudly and Mr. Wallis began to tell the story of the long runs that the dining-cars made without replenishing the food supply. Some of these officials challenged his veracity and he called upon his friends to tell of their own visit to a dining-car kitchen near the end of the usual run without restocking. The inspector at Ogden, Utah, who supplied the cars, continued its service as it had been, and Mr. Wallis countered by confiscating all the suspicious food on all the dining-cars that came over the border into Idaho. But the passengers began to obtain enlightening data about the actual situation. Women's clubs began to send resolutions to the newspapers.

Then the superintendent of the dining-car service came to Idaho on a visit of conciliation and fraternity — anything that Mr. Wallis might suggest the road would be only too glad to put into its plan of operation. And Mr. Wallis was ready with suggestions: inner screen doors for the aisles of the dining-cars and screened windows for the cook's compartment — electric fans, two of them, to play upon the cook's brow and thus discourage perspiration; restocking stations at points along the line so near together that fresh food always could be served. The railroad official readily agreed. Then Mr. Wallis suggested sanitary cots in place of the tables as beds for the waiters, and added that a compartment for the bedding could be built under the floors of the cars so that the bedding need not be stored in the pantry. This plan, too, was agreed on. The final point was that every Pullman porter in the whole train should be equipped with a fly-swatter so that cars from over state lines might not contribute unwelcome additions to Idaho's very scanty fly supply. To-day, a ride in a Pullman car through Idaho is a perfectly sanitary proceeding.

TEACHING BUTCHERS CLEANLINESS

The proprietors of slaughter houses were another group that thought they could resist the demand for the new sanitation. Mr. Wallis looked the slaughter houses over carefully and privately in the dead of night. He wished to find out where the flies went to roost. In doing this he was stretching the provisions of the law, for the national pure food law provides that only food which in itself is tainted can be condemned. There is no reference to the conditions in the plant in which the food is produced. But Mr. Wallis thought that if he could prove that the flies had a chance to roost on the hung quarters of fresh-killed beef, that would be reason enough why the slaughter houses should be torn down and built over.

For several weeks he said nothing while he obtained evidence. His final conclusion was that almost every slaughter house in the state ought to have the torch applied to it and a sanitary, fly-proof building erected in its place. His biggest public move was against a meat company whose plant was located near Boise. Mr. Wallis had been forewarned that he would strike trouble here, for he had heard of a combination among merchants to oppose his work in establishing new standards

Since the facts of business that are necessary to scientific instruction are in many directions actually not known at all, investigation — the discovery and measuring of business facts as a basis for instruction and for the establishing of business principles — became at the outset and has remained one of the dominating traits of the Harvard School.

STANDARDIZING THE SHOE TRADE

The Bureau of Research began its work by investigating the retailing of boots and shoes. This is a widespread branch of retailing, involving big and little stores of every type of management, and dealing in a staple commodity. Business men urged other retail branches for investigation, such as drugs, groceries, and various lines of dry-goods, and one of these businesses has since been taken up. The Bureau of Research sent representatives to study the retail shoe trade in the Middle West, where conditions were considered by those best acquainted with the trade to be broadly typical. The bureau's agents dealt personally with hundreds of retailers, recording the organization, the business conditions, the kind and size of population served, and the dealer's own record of expenses, returns, and profits. The necessity of a uniform system of cost accounting at once became evident. The bureau then drew up an accounting system, and offered to install it for any retailer who would make regular and, of course, confidential returns of his business costs and profits.

Hundreds of shoe retailers, including some of the most important dealers in the largest cities of the country, are now using the Harvard Standard Shoe Cost Accounting System, and making returns to the bureau. From these returns the bureau has been able to determine the "normal" cost, under present methods, of every item of the retail shoe business, for different grades of goods and to some extent for different conditions of population. The coöperating shoe retailer is now able for the first time to compare the various items in his selling expense with the cost of the same items in the business of hundreds of other retailers, and to see where, if at all, he is wasting money.

By this work the Bureau of Business Research has made the Harvard School the first business school to exercise a profound and shaping influence over the conduct of an important branch of "real business" that was established long before the school itself came into existence. Furthermore, through this work of the Bureau of Research, as well as by the collection of many important private business records in its confidential archives, the Harvard School is gathering a body of scientifically verified knowledge of business facts that is unrivaled except by the records of the Federal Government. Here is the foundation of something approaching a "science" of business. It is added to continually by personal investigations that are carried out by the instructors.

BUILDING A SCIENCE OF BUSINESS

That the Harvard School is fulfilling its aim — to teach the profession of business by scientific methods applied to live business material — is made evident by several signs. Its increasing student body, numbering now, in its sixth year, 109, has every year included a notable representation of active business men in executive positions who have come to it for special courses of instruction. The interest of the business world has taken a new form in frequent inquiries from employers concerning men that may be available in the graduating class. Positions are secured for practically all graduates, though the school does not promise this. Every graduate is practically assured of a fair chance to prove his fitness for executive work, and to be put ahead if he "makes good." The professorship of banking and finance has been made permanent by the gift of endowment from a business man, Mr. Edmund C. Converse, of New York. The Harvard Corporation, as well as the business supporters of the school, consider that it has passed from experiment to assured success.

Harvard seems to have found the men, the methods, and the beginning of notable achievement in making the profession of business more scientific and more efficient — in bringing business nearer to its proper place as an applied science.

of sanitation in commerce. To offset the power of the fund which the merchants had raised to defeat him Mr. Wallis employed a very simple expedient — he called in some women.

When he sealed up the plant of the meat company because of the filthy and indescribable conditions that were found at the slaughter house, he was quickly rebuffed. Mr. Wallis then gave the Boise *Capital News* leave to go ahead and print the story of what Mr. Fred. G. Taylor, one of the paper's youngest reporters, had found when he made a secret visit to the company's plant with Mr. Wallis and two women officers of the State Humane Society of Idaho.

The story of what they saw was full of ugly and disagreeable details, but details that aroused the people. The meat concern promptly sued the *Capital News* for libel. Mr. Wallis came to the paper's assistance by asserting the truth of the article and referring to others — including the two women — who could give evidence of its truth. The libel suit was hurried to trial upon the insistence of the defense, and the jury, at the trial's conclusion, took only time enough to draw up a verdict in reporting that the defendant had won. The meat company had got enough of fighting — it learned that it did not pay, and, after its expensive fight, it went out of business.

Mr. Wallis next moved over to a neighboring town and found a hard-working beef, pork, and sheep packer at work on his supply of beeves. Several quarters of dressed meat were hanging in a storage room — covered with roosting flies. The clothing worn by the men was filthy.

"What are you going to slaughter next?" Mr. Wallis asked in his meekest and least belligerent manner.

"The sheep," replied the meat packer, pointing to a pen in which were a dozen fat sheep.

"You might as well spare yourself the trouble," Mr. Wallis remarked, "because I am going to close your place up and burn all the meat I find in the storage room. It isn't fit for the market and isn't going to reach the market."

The meat packer had never heard such

threats before. He could not believe they were in earnest, so he went ahead and killed not only the sheep but a half dozen hogs as well. Next morning Mr. Wallis returned and began to put state seals on the doors of every room in the slaughter house after locking the door shut. He carted off all the carcasses he found in the place and made a bonfire of them. When the proprietor protested he was told he should have acted upon a tip made out of the kindness of the sanitary inspector's heart the night before. But to-day he owns a fly-proof slaughter house in which every appointment is of the latest sanitary design, and all the townspeople point to it with pride. Similar results were achieved in Twin Falls, in Grangeville, and two or three score of other cities.

THE DAIRY CAMERA SQUAD

Mr. Wallis soon found as much to keep him busy in the dairies as he had found in the slaughter houses. The farmers laughed at him a little, so he added a camera-squad to his inspecting force. He took pictures of clean farmhouses and clean dairy-houses and sent them to the newspapers, and other pictures of dirty dairy-houses and dirty farmhouses and sent these to the newspapers, too.

He realized that it would be a long and tedious legal proceeding to force farmers through the courts to keep clean cow barns, whereas the fear of publicity would quickly compel them to do so. The fear of Mr. Wallis's camera-squad became a real one in the rural districts. His pictures of well-kept farms gave ideas to the owners of badly kept farms which they sought to emulate.

For the technical, scientific proofs of evil Mr. Wallis could never gain much respect. Instead of capturing samples of milk and taking them to laboratories to have them tested and then commencing court proceedings after the receipt, days later, of highly technical reports, Mr. Wallis made a simple ruling as to milk. It was that any bottle of milk at the bottom of which sediment could be found would be considered unfit for food. He would sally forth in the early mornings, mount the milk wagons from farms that he knew were conducted without regard for cleanliness, and hunt for sediment in the bottles.

If he found this sediment he would tell the driver to turn around and go back to the farm — carrying the sanitary inspector along as a guest. In the presence of the farmer and his wife Mr. Wallis would dump the milk in the pig pen and tell the farmer that his milk would be treated that way every morning until it was free from sediment.

If the farmers disliked him, the women of the state approved his work with emphasis and nobody arose to dispute Mr. Wallis's ruling. After two years of practice without specific warrant of law, this procedure was given official sanction by the legislature, along with many other reforms that Mr. Wallis had accomplished through the issuance of edicts which had no other backing than the support of the women, a fearless press, and of a constantly enlarging group of enlightened men.

"THE PURE FOOD GRAFTERS"

Mr. Wallis's work of clean-up was opposed in one town by a merchant who posted a big sign in front of his place of business that read, "The Pure Food Grafters Are in Town." Mr. Wallis saw the sign and suggested to the merchant that his work was one that too vitally affected the people to be mocked at. The merchant would not take the sign down so Mr. Wallis had photographs made and sent them to papers in parts of the state where the new standards had ardent support. The merchant heard from the people and from the state's attorney-general in a civil suit for criminal libel, which left him in no doubt as to whether his protest was popular or not. He pleaded guilty before Judge Gwinn, and was heavily fined.

In the beginning of the period in which the tide of public support began to flow in Mr. Wallis's direction, he approached a Federal judge who for years had been sending his prisoners to a certain jail. "That jail's a sad place, Judge Dietrich," said Mr. Wallis, "and I think it would be a fine thing if you sent your prisoners to another county and let me move all that

are now in the jail over the county line as well."

Judge Dietrich agreed to the proposal. District Judge Steele was about to commence a trial before a petit jury in the same county.

LOCKING PRISONERS OUT OF JAIL

"Suppose you invest your petit jury with the inquisitorial powers of a grand jury," suggested Mr. Wallis, "and let them make a tour of inspection with me through the county jail."

The trip was made, the jail condemned, and within an hour every prisoner, whether state or Federal, was on his way to a new jail at Wallace, Ida. Mr. Wallis put locks on the condemned jail to keep prisoners out because it was an unfit place for human beings to inhabit!

When county tax-payers complained because of the expense of keeping prisoners in another county, Mr. Wallis invited them to come with him and look over the jail. After a visit to the place nobody remained who cared to protest. Mr. Wallis burned up every bit of bedding — everything but the steel cages and bare walls of the building itself — before assenting to the return of the prisoners.

The movement spread through every county. Instead of dirty jails in the cellars of court houses, Idaho is now building new jails — and court houses to go with them — the new jails being up on the roofs where the prisoners can always be assured of light and clean air. In the larger counties, where separate jails are needed, the most modern sanitary arrangements are provided.

Mr. Wallis looked over the poor-farm of the state and found the aged men and women sleeping on hard, uncomfortable beds — bought from some man who had made a lower bid than the others in competitive bidding. He declared that one of the purposes of sanitation is to give persons a better chance to live in comfort and that those old people could not live in comfort on the hard beds. The superintendent of the poor-farm did not care to risk an encounter with him. He bought new beds and saw to it that they were built for comfort as well as for stability.

Mr. Wallis found that one of the hardest problems in food reform was to make a pound weigh sixteen ounces. Much of Idaho's butter came in from states that lay to the eastward. A "pound" that weighed more than fifteen ounces was rarely to be found. Mr. Wallis started prosecutions and the dealers replied that they sold their butter by the package and not by the pound. Mr. Wallis appealed to the women again. He asked women in all parts of the state to buy butter — and to obtain receipts showing that their purchase represented so many pounds.

He started prosecutions again and this time, when the familiar defense of the dealers appeared, he exhibited the receipts from all parts of the state. The dealers found they were fighting a much more formidable opponent than Mr. Wallis himself — the aroused housewives of the whole state. Mr. Wallis soon afterward was able to ship large wholesale consignments of butter back to the makers while the dealers in Idaho looked on in meek approval. Butter now comes into Idaho in pound packages of sixteen full ounces.

TWO INSPECTORS IN ONE

The local dealers, when ordered to destroy foodstuffs that were in violation of the law, complained that mail-order houses in the East could compete with local merchants without any such harsh restrictions. Mr. Wallis found the freight warehouse through which mail-order goods were distributed. He put his seals on such goods as he found in the warehouse but the attorneys for the mail-order people immediately threatened injunction proceedings against him on the grounds that he was interfering, as a state officer, with interstate commerce. Mr. Wallis thought things over and took a train for Washington. He told his troubles to the Secretary of Agriculture and received an appointment as a Federal inspector under the pure food law, to work without pay. He also received a box full of Federal seals. In the dark of the first night after he returned to Idaho, he ripped off all his state seals and put Federal seals on the mail-order goods he had seized. He then opened the goods and took samples for bacteriological and chemical analysis.

The mail-order people, of course, sued to make their injunction permanent, but Mr. Wallis replied that they were not dealing with a state inspector at all but with a representative of the National Government who had found baking powder from Chicago with arsenic in it, extracts from New York that were sadly misbranded, coffee from Chicago that was mostly chicory, and "burnt peanuts" from Pennsylvania that were coated with a poisonous shellac. The suit was abandoned, but Mr. Wallis went on to tell the people all that he had found in the mail-order goods: turpentine that had been adulterated with kerosene; lemon extract that contained no lemon juice at all; gall-stone cures that were compounded from a mixture of olive oil and Seidlitz powders!

MISLEADING DRUG LABELS

Next he attacked the dangerous patent medicines. He warned the people in bulletins of the danger in headache cures and of the fact that the amount of heart-depressing drugs stated on the label to be in every wafer was often only a fraction of the amount actually contained. He warned the people, too, that manufacturers were evading the purpose of the law by printing on the labels technical chemical terms for poisons of which the public has become suspicious. He warned them, for example, that on four popular brands of headache cure the coal-tar product "acetanilide" was disguised under the technical designation "phenylacetamide," and that "phenacetin," another coal-tar drug against which the people had frequently been warned, was appearing in headache cures under the new name of "acetphenetidin." The people of Idaho had learned to accept Mr. Wallis's word on other things and they heeded his warnings about impure drugs and fake headache remedies, and the druggists commenced stock-taking and cleaning the banned goods off their shelves.

Mr. Wallis made his annual report for last year a document which the farmer and the merchant alike would read. Handling all sinners with mercy, he still brought forward enough examples of what was good and what was bad practice in every form of commerce to show the buyers what to look for and the sellers what to offer if they would keep public confidence. He illustrated the report with cartoons and photographs until it became a popular book for the fireside rather than a report for state archives.

And by the firesides it is read. Mr. Wallis believes in the public conscience and never tries to move faster than the people will follow him after he has put his case before them. Once the people failed to arouse themselves against a restaurant where he had found boxes of prunes that were worm-eaten and boxes of tea in which spiders had made their nests. He learned that the restaurant was patronized almost entirely by commercial travelers. He carried his case to the commercial travelers at their next state convention and then went with committeemen from that organization through all the restaurants that were patronized by them. The managers might have felt that they could defy Mr. Wallis, but they did not feel that they could defy their own patrons, and they made over their entire plan of kitchen procedure to meet their approval.

A canner in Utah mocked at Mr. Wallis when he told him that his product was too rotten to sell in Idaho. So one day, when Mr. Wallis found some slimy tomatoes in the market in Idaho, he traced them to a wholesale dealer — Mr. Wallis never believed much in punishing the retailers of canned goods.— and through the coöperation of this wholesaler he gathered two carloads of the tomatoes from stores in Idaho and condemned them. The canner in Utah went at once to Boise and asked permission to ship them back to Utah to save the cans and boxes. Mr. Wallis figured that the cans and boxes were not worth it, but the canner insisted, so he consented. When he got back to Utah he gave out an interview in which he said that Mr. Wallis had condemned none of his goods. So Mr. Wallis ripped off his state seals of condemnation and put on Federal seals, believing that, if he let the goods go back to Utah as agreed, they would be made into catsup and sold again. When the canner received the goods in Ogden he found a Federal inspector there to see that every can was actually dumped and destroyed. The canner made a great outcry — but the goods were dumped.

SCHOOL CHILDREN AS SANITARIANS

Mr. Wallis's latest plan is to stir the high school pupils into a vital interest in the problems of municipal sanitation. He has offered three cash prizes for the best essay on how school children can coöperate in the work of keeping Idaho's towns sanitary and clean. The essays are to be read at the graduating exercises next June. Then the winning essay in every school will be sent to the state superintendent of schools and the best three will be chosen for submission to judges who will pick out the best of all. This essay will be published in an edition of more than 125,000 copies and will be distributed by the state to every home in Idaho. Exercises in honor of the winner will be held in every school, and the book will be read as the most important part of the programmes. Three years ago he distributed 75,000 of his famous "Fly Book" to the school children of Idaho.

Mr. Wallis told of his work at the last convention of the Association of State and National Pure Food Inspectors and was promptly elected president of the organization. In this new capacity he is seeking to force amendments to the pure food law which will give Federal inspectors the same jurisdiction over the premises in which food is prepared as they now have over the finished food product and which will make it more difficult for food adulterators to indulge in label-faking and evasion of the law by using strange names instead of well known names for dangerous drugs.

In Idaho, Mr. Wallis has demonstrated again what Dr. Victor Dowling proved in Louisiana, what Dr. Charles T. Nesbitt proved in Wilmington, N. C., and what Dr. John R. Williams proved in Rochester, N. Y. — that a courageous and resourceful public officer can clean up a community or a commonwealth by "dramatizing" his appeal for popular support in such a way that it will get newspaper publicity as well as the respect of the soberminded people who mould public opinion.

Since the facts of business that are necessary to scientific instruction are in many directions actually not known at all, investigation — the discovery and measuring of business facts as a basis for instruction and for the establishing of business principles — became at the outset and has remained one of the dominating traits of the Harvard School.

STANDARDIZING THE SHOE TRADE

The Bureau of Research began its work by investigating the retailing of boots and shoes. This is a widespread branch of retailing, involving big and little stores of every type of management, and dealing in a staple commodity. Business men urged other retail branches for investigation, such as drugs, groceries, and various lines of dry-goods, and one of these businesses has since been taken up. The Bureau of Research sent representatives to study the retail shoe trade in the Middle West, where conditions were considered by those best acquainted with the trade to be broadly typical. The bureau's agents dealt personally with hundreds of retailers, recording the organization, the business conditions, the kind and size of population served, and the dealer's own record of expenses, returns, and profits. The necessity of a uniform system of cost accounting at once became evident. The bureau then drew up an accounting system, and offered to install it for any retailer who would make regular and, of course, confidential returns of his business costs and profits.

Hundreds of shoe retailers, including some of the most important dealers in the largest cities of the country, are now using the Harvard Standard Shoe Cost Accounting System, and making returns to the bureau. From these returns the bureau has been able to determine the "normal" cost, under present methods, of every item of the retail shoe business, for different grades of goods and to some extent for different conditions of population. The coöperating shoe retailer is now able for the first time to compare the various items in his selling expense with the cost of the same items in the business of hundreds of other retailers, and to see where, if at all, he is wasting money.

By this work the Bureau of Business Research has made the Harvard School the first business school to exercise a profound and shaping influence over the conduct of an important branch of "real business" that was established long before the school itself came into existence. Furthermore, through this work of the Bureau of Research, as well as by the collection of many important private business records in its confidential archives, the Harvard School is gathering a body of scientifically verified knowledge of business facts that is unrivaled except by the records of the Federal Government. Here is the foundation of something approaching a "science" of business. It is added to continually by personal investigations that are carried out by the instructors.

BUILDING A SCIENCE OF BUSINESS

That the Harvard School is fulfilling its aim — to teach the profession of business by scientific methods applied to live business material — is made evident by several signs. Its increasing student body, numbering now, in its sixth year, 109, has every year included a notable representation of active business men in executive positions who have come to it for special courses of instruction. The interest of the business world has taken a new form in frequent inquiries from employers concerning men that may be available in the graduating class. Positions are secured for practically all graduates, though the school does not promise this. Every graduate is practically assured of a fair chance to prove his fitness for executive work, and to be put ahead if he "makes good." The professorship of banking and finance has been made permanent by the gift of endowment from a business man, Mr. Edmund C. Converse, of New York. The Harvard Corporation, as well as the business supporters of the school, consider that it has passed from experiment to assured success.

Harvard seems to have found the men, the methods, and the beginning of notable achievement in making the profession of business more scientific and more efficient — in bringing business nearer to its proper place as an applied science.

BORAH, PROGRESSIVES, AND ELECTIONS

This is an interesting discussion of Idaho elections,
Progressive viewpoints and other issues concerning the
political views of the citizens of Idaho.

Source: The Nation, February 23, 1923.

Bill Borah and Other Home Folks
By ANNIE PIKE GREENWOOD

I

Three cheers for the red, white, and blue!
Three cheers for the red, white, and blue!
The army and navy forever—
Three cheers for the red, white, and blue!

THE kitchen door flew open, and the two farmers, in
their "town coats," marched into the room singing
lustily. I, with pancake turner poised, could hardly restrain
myself until their chorus was ended. It was six o'clock
in the morning of the day after election, and the two men
had just returned from an all-night counting of the ballots.
"How did it go?" I cried at the first opportunity.
"We've carried Jerome County, and we may have carried
the State."
"It's too good to be true!" (And it was, about the State!)
But when the returns came in and we found that our man
for governor stood second to the Republican victor, and only
10,000 behind him, we felt justified in declaring: Watch
the Progressive Party in Idaho two years from now. We'll
win next time!

II

The Progressive Party in Idaho is the successor of the
Nonpartisan League. Six years ago the League went into
the Democratic primary and nominated such candidates as
it desired. There was success in so many instances that
we who believed in that for which the League stands felt
so optimistic that we even dreamed of "carrying" the State
in no distant future. But, alas for our hopes, two years
after the entrance of the organized farmers into politics we

fell lamentably behind in the voting. It was the year of the
Republican landslide. I remember one of our good farm
women was passing the bank on election day and, pointing
to a picture of Mr. Harding in the window, she exclaimed
to all who cared to hear: "That face looks good to me!"
And she voted accordingly. And so did they all. The
farmers had suffered so much under the Wilson Administration that they turned with eagerness to a Republican
regime. It never occurred to them that they might experience even greater depression under President Harding.

In our community the farm women organized themselves
into what they call The Ladies' Fancy-work Improvement
Club. Some of the men are ungallant enough to substitute
the word "gossip" for "fancy-work." I was honored by a
request to join, and at the second meeting which I attended,
armed with some socks badly in need of first aid, I heard
the lady who liked Mr. Harding's face complaining bitterly
because her husband could get next to nothing for his crop.
One after another the women joined in the chorus of woe.
At last I jabbed my darning ball with my needle, blunting it
thereby, and turning to the Harding lady I addressed her:
"Didn't I understand you to say that you voted the Republican ticket this year?"

"I did," she answered, "and I'm proud of it. Pa always
voted the Republican ticket, and his Pa before him. We've
all been Republicans in our family, and always will."

"My father was always a Democrat," spoke up another
woman. "I expect to vote the Democratic ticket till I die."

"Me, too. Our family was always Democratic."

"Well, our family back as far as we can trace was always
Republican."

At last I struck in: "Then don't complain any more about
the price your farm products brought. What did you do
to change conditions for the farmer? You helped make the
world safe for the business man, the banker, and you left
the farmer and his muddled affairs entirely out, just as the
old parties intended that you should do. I suppose I am
the only woman present who voted for the Nonpartisan
candidates."

"No," spoke one little woman, "I voted for the Non-
partisans, too. Henry made me!"

"Hurrah for Henry!" said I.

Now, the significant part of this defeat for the farmer
vote is this: in spite of the fact that we did not win anything to speak of, we actually gained ten thousand votes

more than we had the first year. Slowly—slowly—do you see it creeping?

III

When I received notice that I had been chosen as clerk of the Progressive primary I was dismayed, but I took my courage in my hands, and what was equally important, tried to see if I could do a day's work in one morning, so that the machinery of the house could go on without me.

When we came to Idaho from Kansas we brought a buggy. This vehicle passed away, and we purchased a "white top" or "Mormon hack," our family having grown. This, too, went the way of the "one hoss shay." We now bought a two-wheel cart for the convenience of our son Walter, to ride to high school, six miles away. This vehicle has continued to act as our means of communication with the town. With Florry harnessed to this, my eleven-year-old boy Charles and I set out for Hazelton.

Florry is a farm horse. She is so big, and the cart so small, that she almost sat in our laps as we sped along. The road over which we usually went was like a river of flour, the dust was so deep. So Charles and I decided to take the desert road, up across the railroad track, out through the sage-brush where our only encounters would be with jack-rabbits and coyotes. But, oh, that lava rock! When that extinct crater north of us belched forth red-hot stones and liquid fire I am sure that it was with no future design against our rickety cart and our resentful Florry, who stubbornly refused to tread upon even the smallest stone, and was forever bouncing our cart from one black eminence to another. Then there was the stream under the railroad trestle, with two boards across it for the wheels, but nothing for the horse. Florry was bound she would "walk the plank" and send us into the stream. Poor Charles see-sawed his arms until he was exhausted, pulling at the reins to keep her straight. We crossed, and immediately entered into a long, uphill quagmire of mud, the waste-water seepage from the farm through which we were compelled to pass. Over the railroad track, across the condemned bridge with the foaming, racing water underneath. When a bridge becomes dangerous to human life the county officials nail up a board with the word "Condemned" in big letters. There the responsibility ends. If you cross, and the bridge suddenly gives way, your death is on your own head. And then it is time to build a new bridge.

Upon reaching Hazelton I went to the drug-store to ask

where the Progressive primary might be. I was told that it was probably in the hotel. I crossed the street to that homely edifice, and entered the front door. Several of our local business men were seated at a long table, and one of them advanced toward me smiling and rubbing his hands together unctuously. All the other men smiled and spoke to me. The man who had come to meet me asked: "Did you come to vote, Mrs. Greenwood?"

"I was looking for the Progressive primary," I answered.

Talk about an eclipse of the sun! It was as though some-one had called, "lights out!" Every blind went down in those faces. A frigid voice answered: "I think you'll find it further up the street."

I did. A farmer, whom I knew slightly, was there before me. He informed me that he was a judge of the election. He had the books in his keeping. We waited an hour for other officials to appear. Since they did not, we swore each other in as clerk and judge and every other necessary officer. And there we waited. We had one voter that entire day. Is it any wonder that I did not have faith that the Progressive Party would make much impression on election day? Of course, I overlooked somewhat the fact that there was no contest in our primary, all candidates having been chosen in advance, while nearly every office was being hotly contested in the Republican primary, and almost as much so in the Democratic primary. The next day one of our farm men went to town. When he returned he said: "Your Pro-gressive primary is the laughing-stock of the town." "Let them laugh," I answered. It was mere bravado on my part, for in my secret heart I did not believe the Progres-sives would make any showing. "You know the farmers," I had been told so many times. "They won't stick."

IV

For the first time in the history of our segregation there were political rallies in the schoolhouse. The first to come were the Progressives. I was the only woman present at that rally. I looked at that room filled with farmers in their old mackinaws or sheepskin coats and overalls, and I won-dered whether it would not be more lady-like for me to trot back home, but as a voter I decided to remain.

I do not use perfect English myself, as you have no doubt discovered by this time, and yet I have always cringed at certain incorrect expressions, and have been inclined to underestimate anyone using them. But on this night I listened to language which had heretofore turned me against

the speakers, and I was not turned. I heard those earnest
men talking straight from their hearts and out of their
hard experiences. The candidates present that night were
all farmers except one man, a carpenter. Said one speaker:
"The Republicans and the Democrats have each a sure
remedy for what ails the farmer. The Republicans say that
all that is the matter with you is that you are overburdened
with taxes, and that when they are cut down you will be
in a prosperous condition. How many of you men here
tonight have paid your taxes?" Not a hand went up.
"Then," continued the speaker, "if you have not paid your
taxes, you should be prosperous, but since you are not, then
the taxes can't be the big problem. The Democrats say
that all that is the matter with the farmer is that he should
raise more cows and hogs, and quit raising hay and grain.
You farmers know what would happen if we all went into
raising hogs and cows. Then when the smash came the
Democrats would say that all the farmer needs is to quit
raising cows and hogs and raise more hay and grain."

An appeal was made to us to vote the straight Progressive
ticket. "Better vote for a poor man who believes as you
do than a good man who believes in the opposite principles,
for the good man can do more harm by reason of his greater
efficiency and his wrong belief than the poor man can do
when he is trying his best to do what you believe is right."
I was convinced. I had voted a scratched ticket always,
contending that I voted for men and not parties; that good
men were the important thing, no matter what their belief.
I resolved never to scratch my ticket again.

Shortly after this the Democrats arrived. The farmers
all went, as they had agreed to attend the rallies of all
parties. Soon afterward the Republicans came and, canniest
of all, they brought with them buns, wienerwursts, and hot
coffee. And our Progressive men were kind enough to eat
all the refreshments provided while making the Republican
candidates for the legislature squirm under their questions.

V

The greatest sensation of the campaign was the spectacu-
lar entrance into Idaho of Senator William T. Borah. We
heard his thunderous approach from afar, and it is not too
much to say that upon his advent Idaho stood up on her
hind legs and howled, both with delight and with derision.
He stumped the State from one end to the other, defying the
Republican machine of his home State; condemning the
present cabinet form of government and the State con-

stabulary; coming out flat-footed for the direct primary in
spite of the convention plank in the Republican platform;
splitting his party wide open, and not giving a care; chal-
lenging Moore, the Republican candidate for Governor, to
reject the Republican platform, and make one of his own.

I had been bitterly opposed to Borah for many reasons,
chief among them being his stand on woman suffrage. It
seemed to me that he was dashing around in Congress with
bumptious conceit, his eye fixed on the Presidential chair.
But soon I began to read accounts of remarks like these:

"I defy the whole outfit." (The Republican "regulars" were
attacking him.) "I don't propose to go back to the United States
Senate at the suggestion of the organization. I don't even ask
their consent to go back to the Senate of the United States."

"If I was in Charley Moore's place I would kick that platform into the dust-heap and I would tell the people of this State,
regardless of the platform, what I was going to do."

"I want the Republican Party, but I want it right. . . . Now,
before the twentieth of October let us have a program."

"The next two years belong to me—nobody but God Almighty
can take them away from me, and during that period I am
going to say precisely what I think, and advocate the policies
in which I believe, regardless of the political consequences to
the Republican Party."

Since these reports came from machine Republican papers,
I wondered what the truth might be. I wanted to hear
Borah, and the opportunity came. I was included in a party
to go by automobile to Twin Falls, twenty-seven miles away.
We left the ranch at 5:30 and when we reached Twin Falls
we went immediately to the hall where Senator Borah was
to speak. We had eaten no supper, but we were glad that
we had not delayed, for an immense crowd had gathered
before the closed doors, and we were lucky to find a place in
line. I had heard that half the people who went to hear him
were unable to gain admittance. It took less than fifteen
minutes after the doors were opened to fill the hall and
overflow the stage. All sorts of people were there, mostly
middle-aged, prosperous-looking, white-collared business
men and their wives, and weather-beaten farmers with their
serious-looking mates. And then came the great Borah,
with his "old-fashioned hair-cut," as one man put it.

He talked quietly and convincingly, without oratory. He
told us of our over-officered army—as bad as a Mexican
army; of the ship subsidy and its injustice; of the Federal
Reserve and the enormous salaries of its officials; of the de-
plorable war debt, and the despairingly long time it will take

to pay it; he spoke in favor of the direct primary, as I had been told he would, and condemned the extravagance of the cabinet form of government; and last, and most emphatically, he declared that both old parties must clean house and offer something the people want, or the people will take things into their own hands and form a third party.

After it was over we went to a restaurant. Seated at one of the tables were some Borah-Republicans who accosted me. "What did you think of him, Mrs. Greenwood?" I answered: "If the Republican Party would follow Borah, there would be no need for a Progressive Party."

And right here I make this statement: I thoroughly believe that *Senator William E. Borah made more votes for the Progressive Party than any other man.*

VI

I got out of my bed, where I was ill with bronchitis, to go to Hazelton to register. I would have risen from my death-bed to register and vote. The following Monday was election day. I had been sick for over a week, and I simply had to do the washing. There is no way of disposing of the laundry on a ranch except by washing it, unless you can afford to make a bonfire of it. My neighbors had promised to take me to town to vote. Word came to me that they were ready, and I left the suds in the middle of the washing, donned street clothes, and joined them. We passed all sorts of vehicles, from automobiles to farm wagons, on their way to Hazelton, and we met many automobiles coming back to take more voters into town, having already performed that office many times. There was Ben Temple driving a borrowed automobile with the tatters of his sheepskin coat fluttering in the wind. That sheepskin coat seemed symbolic to me. Every year when Ben planted his crop he said "This year I'll get a new sheepskin coat," and every year the crop not only failed to pay for a new sheepskin coat, but it failed to pay even for itself. And each year the coat grew more ragged and Ben grew more determined to see what he could do by way of the vote to change conditions. On this particular election day he was taking in voters by the scores, and there was nothing in it for him but the satisfaction of doing it. And there was Frank Melotte. We passed him in his automobile returning for more voters, as he had been doing all day, his eyes set and serious, a returned volunteer soldier, who is once again a volunteer fighting the farmer's battle. When I reached town I saw farmers—farmers everywhere, and their wives with them. How could I tell

they were farmers? In the words of Ben Temple, "If you
see a man and he's got a fairly good suit and coat, why,
that's a tramp; if you see a man in a ragged coat and worn-
out overalls, that's a farmer." And their wives. Hats and
coats of the vintage of 1912, and raw red hands, and
anxious, toil-worn faces. A baby in arms and one in the
man's arms, clothed in worn old things, cut down. Where
is the folding go-cart that could have been brought to town
so handily? The dream of it is buried out in the field with
the frozen potatoes. They who feed the world, looking like
beggars, and feeling far worse than beggars!

I was in the voting-booth just long enough to make an ✕.
I came out and seated myself on a bench where I could
watch the voters come and go. The farmers and their
wives came through the street door, entered the booths,
and came out, in about the time that it is taking me to tell
this. My heart rejoiced. I felt that they were voting the
Progressive ticket straight.

But I was not prepared for the returns. Our candidate
was only ten thousand votes behind the Republican candidate, and far outstripped the Democratic candidate. Here
again is the important fact: Two years ago we gained ten
thousand votes more than at our first campaign, and *this
year we gained another ten thousand votes. We need now
only a matter of five thousand and one votes to make Idaho a
Progressive State.* And we'll have them two years from
now. Our campaign is already begun. Not slowly any
more, but by one bound!

VII

The preamble of the Progressive Party platform makes a
clear and definite statement of belief. Many will read the
following lines with horror, but I venture to prophesy that
they will see every principle here set down incorporated into
the platforms of one or another and perhaps both of the old
parties before much time has passed.

We, the delegates to the State Convention of the Progressive
Party in Idaho assembled at Nampa, August 22, 1922, declare
the paramount issue is the abolition of privilege, meaning by
privilege the unjust economic advantage by possession of which
a small group controls our natural resources, transportation,
industry, and credit; stifles competition; prevents equal opportunity of development for all; and thus dictates the conditions
under which we live.

We are against coalition with any political party, and pledge
that not one of our State candidates will withdraw in favor of
any candidate in either of the old parties. We advocate:

1. A State-wide open primary law and a sound, workable initiative, referendum, and recall.

2. Public control of natural resources; just taxation of all land values, including land containing coal, oil, mineral deposits, large water powers, and large commercial timber tracts, in order to prevent monopoly. We favor the gradual exemption from taxation of the products of labor and industry.

3. Public ownership and operation of railroads and enough public utilities to compete with monopoly.

4. Equal rights for all citizens: free speech, free press, and free assembly for lawful purposes, as guaranteed in the Constitution.

5. State efficiency and tax reduction by the abolishment of the State constabulary, the cabinet form of government, and other tax-eating, useless commissions; the reformation of the State highway and game departments, and the election of the State utilities commission.

6. A State graduated inheritance tax and income tax on incomes over $5,000—like the Wisconsin law.

7. A guaranty bank deposit law.

8. The well-known and just demands of labor, including an exclusive State fund compensation act similar to the Ohio law.

9. An impartial enforcement of all laws, including the prohibition law.

10. Laws to protect individual and cooperative enterprise from monopoly.

11. A national soldier bonus, paid for by tax on excess profits.

12. Money control to be taken from the private monopoly of the Federal Reserve system and restored to the national government.

13. We pledge ourselves to take the judiciary out of politics.

VIII

You will wonder whether H. F. Samuels, our choice for Governor, is a farmer, as was Senator Frazier of North Dakota. Mr. Samuels came to northern Idaho to practice law, which he did so successfully that he became a county prosecuting attorney. He became interested in the mining of that part of our State, and perfected a process for the extraction of zinc from low-grade ore, and was consequently known as "the Zinc King." During the war he answered the government's appeal for more agricultural produce by turning thousands of acres of logged-off land into cultivated fields. It was while engaged in this occupation that he first became interested in the Nonpartisan League. He was so much interested, in fact, that he went to North Dakota to investigate for himself. He became an ardent member, and the result was his selection as candidate for Governor by the Nonpartisan League two years ago. This

year he was our candidate again, and the election shows
that he ran way ahead of his ticket.

IX

Every cause has its martyrs, and the martyrs are not all
dead. There is one man in Idaho to whom the farmers are
more indebted than to any other man. For their cause he
has been persecuted, his wife socially ostracized, his children made to weep bitter tears by their jeering schoolmates.

Ray McKaig was a minister in a certain church in Milwaukee. He married a girl who was a teacher of English
in a college. That sounds like a perfectly respectable beginning, doesn't it? But note how they fell. Mr. McKaig
was warned by his physician that he was consumptive, and
must live out of doors. He and his wife decided to take up
a homestead in North Dakota.

The next chapter finds them shingling the roof of their
little house on the plains of North Dakota. There they
were, bride and groom, both busy with hammer and nails,
and little dreaming that the cloud of dust coming up the
road was Destiny approaching. The cloud of dust stopped
at the McKaig farm gate, and a man came out of its en-
veloping gray. Coming near the two on the roof he introduced himself as the tax collector. "How many cows have
you?" "How many horses?" and so on, until he asked, "How
much did this house cost you?"

"You are surely not going to tax me for this house," said
Mr. McKaig, in astonishment.

"I certainly am."

"But, man, when I made these improvements I made more
valuable those hundreds of acres of idle land next to my
farm, which are being held for speculation. I made this
country a better place to live by improving my farm. You
are not taxing me; you are fining me!"

But he had to pay it just the same, just as all we farmers
have to pay for every step toward greater decency that we
make. It set him thinking. Plowing is an ideal occupation when a man has something on his mind. Only if he
has it on his mind hard enough he is apt to do just as Ray
McKaig did; he will leave the plow in the furrow and go out
and raise his voice against injustice.

Ray McKaig joined the Nonpartisan League, and the
voice that had exhorted worshipers to turn to God, now
began to call to farmers to look to the government. Ray
McKaig is an inspired speaker, deep, logical, interesting,
witty. There are few who can compare with him. The
State Federation of Agriculture of Idaho, including farmers, cattle men, sheepmen, and all others in any way interested in agriculture, invited Ray McKaig to address their
big convention, at which many prominent men were to
speak, Governor Alexander being one. Mr. McKaig spoke
to such effect that the farmers present immediately organized and joined the Nonpartisan League.

BASIC FACTS

Capital: Boise.
Largest City: Boise.
Nicknames: Gem State; Gem of the Mountains.
Song: "Here We Have Idaho."
Abbreviation: ID

43rd State to enter Union, July 3, 1890.
Area: 83,557 sq. mi.
Population (1970 Census): 718,000

State Tree: Western White Pine.

State Bird: Mountain Bluebird.

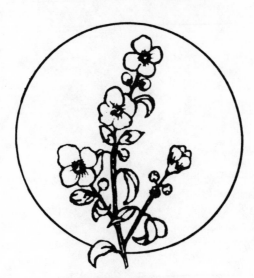

State Flower: Syringa.

Congressional Districts of Idaho

Congressional Districts of Idaho

SELECTED BIBLIOGRAPHY

Barber, Floyd R. and Dan W. Martin. Idaho in the Pa-
    cific Northwest. Caldwell, Idaho: The Caxton
    Printers, Ltd., 1956

Beal, Merrill D. A History of Southeastern Idaho.
    Caldwell, Idaho: The Caxton Printers, Ltd., 1942

Defenbach, Byron. The State We Live In, Idaho. Cald-
    well, Idaho: The Caxton Printers, Ltd., 1933.

Donaldson, Thomas Korwin. Idaho of Yesterday. Caldwell,
    Idaho: The Caxton Printers, Ltd., 1941.

Elsensohn, Alfreda. Pioneer Days in Idaho County. Cald-
    well, Idaho:The Caxton Printers, Ltd., 1947.

French, Hiram Taylor. History of Idaho; A Narrative
    Account of Its Historical Progress, Its People and
    Its Principal Interests. 3 vols. Chicago and New
    York: The Lewis Publishing Company, 1914.

Hailey, John. The History of Idaho. Boise,Idaho: Press
    of Syms-York Company, Inc., 1910.

Hawley, James H. History of Idaho, The Gem of the
    Mountains. 4 vols. Chicago: The S. J. Clarke Pub-
    lishing Company, 1920.

An Illustrated History of North Idaho. N.P.:Western
    Historical Publishing Company, 1903.

Kallenbach, Joseph E. and Jessamine S. Kallenbach.
    American State Governors, 1776-1976. 3 vols.
    Dobbs Ferry, N. Y.: Oceana Publications, Inc.,
    1977-

Livingston-Little, Dallas E. An Economic History of
    North Idaho. Los Angeles: Journal of the West,
    1965.

McConnell, William John. Early History of Idaho. Cald-
    well, Idaho: The Caxton Printers, Ltd., 1913.

Rees, John E. Idaho Chronology, Nomenclature, Bibliog-
    raphy. Chicago: W. B. Conkey Co., 1918.

NAME INDEX

Alexander, Moses, 9
Andrus, Cecil D., 13

Baldridge, H. Clarence, 10
Ballard, David W., 3
Bann, William M., 5
Benewa, Chief, 9
Bennett, Thomas W., 4
Bingham, Henry Harrison, 5
Blaine, James G., 6
Bonner, Edwin L., 7
Bonneville, Benjamin Louis
  Eulalie de, 8
Bottolfsen, Clarence A.,
  10
Brady, James H., 7

Clark, Barzilla W., 10
Clark, Chase A., 10
Clark, Sam, 9
Clark, William, 3, 8
Custer, George Armstrong,
  5

Davis, David W., 9
Donaldson, Thomas, 4

Elmore, Ida, 5

Fairchild, Caribou, 9
Fremont, John C., 6

Garfield, James A., 6
Gilson, Horace C., 3
Goodring, Frank R., 7, 8
Gossett, Charles C., 11

Haines, John M., 8
Hardin, J. S., 3
Harrison, Benjamin, 6
Hawley, James H., 7
Hayes, Rutherford B., 4
Haywood, James H., 7
Hill, Jerome, 1
Howlett, S. R., 2
Hunt, Frank W., 7

Irwin, John N., 5

Jefferson, Thomas, 8
Jordan, Len B., 11
Joseph, Chief, 4

Kaufman, William, 2

Lewis, Meriwether, 1, 8
Lincoln, Abraham, 1, 6
Lootens, Rt. Rev. Louis, 3,
  4
Lyon, Caleb Lyon, 2

Madison, James, 8
McConnell, William J., 6
McCrary, George W., 4
Moore, Charles C., 10
Morris, Joseph, 2
Morrison, John T., 7
Mullan, Joseph, 1

Neil, John B., 5

Payette, Francis, 9

Richards, Franklin Dewey,
  8
Riggs, Ada, 2
Riggs, H. C., 2
Robins, Charles A., 17
Ross, C. Ben, 10

Samuelson, Don, 12
Schwatka, Frederick G., 2
Shoup, George L., 5, 6
Simmons, Frederick H., 2
Smith, C. de Witt, 2
Smylie, Robert E., 11, 12
Spalding, Henry, 1
Steptoe, Col. Edward Jenner,
  1
Steunenberg, Frank, 6, 7
Stevenson, Edward A., 5

Thompson, D. P., 4

Wallace, William H., 2
Wassoon, Joseph, 2
Washington, George, 4
Wiley, Norman B., 6
Williams, Arnold, 11
Wright, Col. George, 1